50
GREATEST
GOLF LESSONS
of the CENTURY

50 GREATEST GOLF LESSONS of the CENTURY

PRIVATE SESSIONS WITH THE GOLF GREATS

JOHN JACOBS

with STEVE NEWELL

Illustrations by RODGER TOWERS

HarperCollins*Publishers*

For me to embark on this book, when my life is still blessedly busy, could have only happened when a persuasive and very able co-author appeared on the scene. Enter Steve Newell. After John Stobbs, Ken Bowden, Dick Aultman, Laddie Lucas and Peter Dobereiner – friends and co-authors of previous books – Steve had a hard act to follow. But how lucky can one get? I found him tremendous. His wide knowledge and intelligent grasp of the game ensured me a first-class interpreter of all that I wanted to say. These greats of golf are his heroes, too. Thanks Steve.

JOHN JACOBS

50 GREATEST GOLF LESSONS OF THE CENTURY.
Copyright © 1999 by John Jacobs.
All rights reserved. Printed in the United States of America. No part of this book may be used or reproduced in any manner whatsoever without written permission except in the case of brief quotations embodied in critical articles and reviews.

For information address HarperCollins*Publishers*, Inc.,
10 East 53rd Street, New York, New York 10022.

HarperCollins books may be purchased for educational, business, or sales promotional use. For information, please write to:
Special Markets Department, HarperCollins Publishers, Inc.,
10 East 53rd Street, New York, New York 10022.

Designed and produced by
Cooling Brown, Middlesex, England

Colour reproduction by Colourscan, Singapore
Printed and bound in Italy

ISBN 0-06-271614-X

FIRST EDITION
99 01 02 03 04 HCUK 10 9 8 7 6 5 4 3 2 1

Contents

John Jacobs: *a lifetime in golf*

John Jacobs started his professional golfing life in his father's shop at Lindrick Golf Club in Yorkshire. He would stoke fires in the grate on Monday mornings to burn out snapped hickory shafts of clubs broken over the course of a weekend's play. He grew up to become one of golf's most influential figures. Tournament winner, founder of the PGA European Tour, Ryder Cup player and twice captain of the team, OBE and President of the PGA of Europe; his accolades and achievements are a tribute to his many gifts on and off the golf course.

Above all, though, John is one of the most distinguished and experienced teachers the game of golf has ever known. He is a prolific and best-selling author and co-founder of the John Jacobs Golf Schools – currently the biggest and most successful golf schools in the world. His teaching methods have inspired millions of club golfers around the world and his keen eye for the swing, astute diagnosis and skilful way with words mean that for more than 50 years he has been constantly in demand by many of the world's great players. To them, John is a rare breed indeed – a proven tournament winner who also happens to be a brilliant teacher.

John remembers very clearly the season of his transformation from tour pro to teacher. "I never wanted to be a teacher," he says. "I wanted to be the best player in the world. But within six months of quitting the tour to concentrate on teaching, I knew I'd made the right decision. I was a happy person again. I didn't have the frustrations of trying to become the best player. Instead I was content with believing I was the best teacher."

There has never been any shortage of golfers willing to confirm this belief and many of golf's greatest names consider it a stroke of good fortune that John chose the career path he did, as is clear from the following tributes.

JOSE MARIA OLAZABAL

"John is the nicest person I have met in my 25-year amateur and professional career, he really is a true friend. As a golf teacher he is without doubt 'The Master'. Simplicity is the word I would use to describe his teaching. His theories on the golf swing and the lessons he gives are so crystal-clear and understandable that he makes the game of golf seem easy. His advice helps bring better golf within everyone's grasp."

GARY PLAYER

"John Jacobs has been a friend of mine for many years, in fact since the mid-1950s when I first played golf in the UK. We co-designed the Edinburgh Course at the Wentworth Club in London and we have exchanged many thoughts on the golf swing. He is an outstanding teacher. John has also been an excellent golfer and fierce competitor on the course. However, of greatest importance for me is that he is a true gentleman and an asset to the game."

DAVID LEADBETTER

"John Jacobs has contributed a great deal to the game and he is considered one of golf's premier teachers. In building my own career as a teacher, he was certainly one of the instructors that I studied and he has an outstanding ability to analyze golfers' problems through their ball-flight. John was the first teacher to discuss the ball-flight laws which enabled teachers to make simple corrections for pupils without getting into detailed theory. He was a master at being able to watch a person hit a shot and then give the necessary fix, more often than not being very successful. His playing skills, Ryder Cup captaincy and golf course architectural

achievements, all combined with his teaching ability have made him one of the game's real grandmasters."

As John's collaborator I can only add to those comments my own thoughts on what a privilege it has been to work with him on this project. I have to say that in our many meetings together to discuss all of the marvellous players featured in this book, I have been enthralled by his anecdotes involving golf's truly legendary figures from past and present and enlightened by his knowledge of the

Jose Maria Olazabal hits balls under John's watchful gaze at the 1997 Ryder Cup, a routine that has paid dividends as far back as the Spaniard's amateur days, up to him becoming a double-Masters champion.

golf swing. What is also abundantly clear is that in an ever-changing game John's teaching methods have remained the same for 50 years and that they are as true, logical and correct today as they have ever been. Moreover, he speaks a language that golfers of every ability can absorb and benefit from. John says: "Being able to help people is I think what it comes down to, suggesting a few things here and there and really seeing the difference. I count myself lucky to have been able to do that and it's always been a pleasure to me." As you read this book I hope you'll agree that the pleasure is, in fact, all ours.

STEVE NEWELL

The flight of the ball reveals all

Before we start examining the swings of the greatest, here are a few of my philosophies on the golf swing.

The nature of every single shot you hit is determined by what the clubhead is doing when it meets the golf ball. Therefore the quality of your golf swing is measured not by aesthetics, but how well it delivers the clubhead to the ball. This is where golf's four impact factors come into play. These factors lie at the heart of my whole teaching philosophy and crop up regularly in the lessons I've given to the golfing greats, so it makes sense to explain these to you before we go any further.

Clubhead Swing Path: Certainly with straight-faced clubs this is the factor that has the most influence on the initial direction of ball-flight. If the ball starts on target, regardless of whether it then deviates left or right through the air, you can be sure that the clubhead was travelling on the correct swing path at impact. If the ball shoots off the clubface immediately in the wrong direction, then your swing path is not on line. An out-to-in swing path starts the ball left of target and an in-to-out swing path starts the ball right of target.

Clubhead Angle of Attack: This is directly linked to the path of your swing. If you swing from out-to-in, you will tend to swing the clubhead into the ball on a steep angle of attack. If you swing from in-to-out, you will generate a more sweeping angle of attack, perhaps even hitting the ball on the upswing.

The position of the ball in your stance also influences the clubhead's angle of attack into impact. Normally if the ball is back in your stance, the clubhead will make contact with it relatively early in the downswing arc and thus be travelling down quite steeply. If the ball is forward in your stance, then contact is made quite late in the downswing arc and the angle of attack is thus more shallow, even slightly on the upswing. It is for these reasons that correct ball position is so vital.

Clubface Alignment: This is the most important of the four impact factors. Incorrect clubface alignment at impact imparts unwanted sidespin. A clubface that is closed to the swing path produces hook spin. A clubface that is open produces slice spin. The trouble is, these bad shots cause you to make compensations in your set-up and swing, which means that if you play with an incorrectly aligned clubface for very long, you effectively start to groove swing faults. This is not a good scenario.

Clubhead Speed: This, the final impact factor, is totally dependent on the previous three. You can swing the club as hard and fast as you like, but if you don't bring together the other three elements you won't generate effective clubhead speed and you won't hit the ball very far. However, if you successfully combine clubhead swing path, angle of attack and clubface alignment, you will maximize your effective clubhead speed and hit the ball further. You have my personal guarantee on that.

This is why the golf ball is a very honest teacher. It doesn't lie or mislead you, it tells you immediately what the clubhead was doing as you swung it through impact. If you understand the visual messages that your ball is telling you, then you can begin to trace them back to your swing. I believe that if you analyze your game in this way, you will start to understand the workings of your swing and get the most out of this book.

But I like to think this is more than just an instruction manual. It charts the evolution of the golf swing and how the game has been played throughout the 20th century. More importantly, in analyzing each of the wonderful players featured, I have highlighted for you exactly why they were so good and what you can learn from their game. Believe me, we can all learn from the best in the world – the key is knowing which bits are best for you. That's what a book like this can give you, the knowledge and the inspiration to experiment. I remember as a boy reading something and jumping out of my seat and trying it, seeing if it felt any better than what I already did. That fascination and curiosity has never left me and there is no doubt in my mind it is one of the reasons I became a good player and a successful teacher.

As you apply my theories to your game, always be aware of what the ball is doing and understand that everything you strive to achieve in your swing must be directed towards making a better impact. Without that objective, your entire game becomes little more than a hit-and-hope experience. Trust me. With the knowledge I've gained through teaching this wonderful game, combined with your golf ball's brutal honesty and the techniques of some of golf's greatest golfers, I think we make a great team. I sincerely hope you enjoy the book and above all that it helps you become a better player.

JOHN JACOBS

Seve Ballesteros

With his Latin dark good looks and film-star smile, Seve always did have a natural ability to attract attention. But when he had a golf club in his hands there were times when his magical influence seemingly made the whole world sit up and take notice.

When Seve arrived on the scene in the late 1970s it was like the circus had come to town. Massive galleries hung on his every move, waiting for his next logic-defying stunt or Houdini-like display of escapology. Here was a man playing the game in a way not witnessed since Arnold Palmer in the early 1960s. Suddenly, golf wasn't merely a sport – it was theatre. Seve could shoot 65 a hundred different ways and every one would be mesmerizing and compelling to watch.

Even now I'm often reminded of the first time I saw Seve. He would have been about 16 years of age. I watched him hit shots and said: "My God, there's talent if ever I saw it, but he'll have to careful. He'll get back trouble if he keeps on swinging like that." That proved to be quite prophetic. He was too much 'under' in the hitting area, which is particularly hard on the back. His ferocious swing down and through the ball was enough to make you almost wince in pain! But there was greatness in him,

all right, and he didn't take long to show us all just how great he was. Within a few years he'd virtually won the Open and by the time he was 21 he'd topped the European money list three year's running. A remarkable feat for one so young.

When he did win his first Open, at Royal Lytham in 1979, I followed him for the whole of that final round. It was a windy day and the course was playing hard and fast. Everyone was having a job hitting the fairways and that's why I'm sure Seve made a conscious decision to just hit the ball off the tee as hard as he could. He smashed it miles, but invariably missed fairways on the 'correct' side. The 16th was a good example. That hole was playing into a left-to-right wind and the pin was tucked behind a bunker on the front-left corner of the green. Even from the middle of the fairway there was no shot at the pin. Seve launched the ball on the wind and it finished in the infamous car park, almost pin high on the right, from where he had a simple pitch against the wind from the perfect line in. All that business about him being lucky and calling him the 'car park champion' is nonsense – I think he knew what he was doing all along.

Shortly afterwards, during the build-up to the 1980 US Masters, an American magazine predicted that Seve couldn't win at Augusta until he learnt to drive the ball. I disagreed and so did Fuzzy Zoeller. Fuzzy had played in the Pro Celebrity series at Gleneagles with Seve and said: "This boy is a genius. He can win anywhere." Seve proved us right that year and won the Masters at a canter. He was a far better driver than that panel of experts realized – very long and not nearly as wild as some believed. In any case, Augusta is not narrow off the tee and rough was non-existent then. But the fast,

heavily contoured greens represented the perfect stage on which Seve could act out his vast repertoire of exquisite short shots.

Believe me, his short game is as good as the legend has it. There's a softness, mixed with authority, in the sublime way he plays his shots. The chip from the back of the green at Lytham in 1988, to wrap-up his third Open title, was a classic display of this great art. I also remember one occasion in America when Ben Crenshaw and Jack Nicklaus watched Seve as he practiced hitting shots out of a bunker with every club from a nine-iron to four-wood. At the height of his powers, his short game was like something from another planet.

There's no doubt in my mind that Seve completely changed the whole face of European golf. At a time when Americans were dominating both the majors and the Ryder Cup, Seve swung the momentum Europe's way. He genuinely believed he was invincible and his whole demeanour oozed self-confidence and pride.

The mid-to-late 1990s were not so kind to Seve. His spine finally succumbed to the years of abuse his swing had inflicted on it and, whereas he once buzzed with confidence, the increasing number of missed fairways and greens seemed to visibly chip away at his self-belief. But it is neither right nor appropriate to dwell on Seve's loss of form, when instead we should applaud him for the way he played the game and thank him for the wonderful memories. For sheer entertainment value he was in a different stratosphere. I for one feel privileged to have witnessed him at his best.

1: Imagination is the key to creativity

DIAGNOSIS: It's part of the Seve legend that he learnt to play golf with just one club – a cut-down three-iron. This 'private education' taught him all the skills that eventually became the hallmarks of his game – superb clubhead control, great feel, touch and above all, imagination. It's part of the reason Seve has been such a joy to watch over the years. He can see shots that others would scarcely dream of and play shots that others wouldn't even contemplate. It's a rare talent.

EXPLANATION: Seve's early experience of golf reminds me of my own boyhood at Lindrick Golf Club in the 1930s, where a few of us invented a little chipping course at the back of the caddie shed. We used to go round it so many times there was hardly ever any grass on it. We had just one club, a hickory version of a four-iron, and learnt how to manufacture all kinds of different shots with it. I got so confident and so 'sharp' that I never dreamed of mis-hitting the ball, even off the scrappiest of lies.

Many years later when I was teaching national teams at La Manga in Spain, I used to lay out a nine-hole chipping course around the putting green and teach the same philosophy. I would nominate various clubs from a sand-wedge to a three-iron and make everyone chip on to the green with whatever club I gave them.

CORRECTION: This is a wonderful way to learn about the short game and develop great touch and feel. Don't ever stand on the practice ground, placing every ball on a perfect lie and chip balls to the same flag. It doesn't take a genius to knock those shots close. You have to challenge yourself with tough lies or you'll never improve. What you'll soon find, I'm sure, is that you learn to visualize shots in your mind and develop the touch and the feel to turn them into reality. That's what a great short game is all about.

Whenever you practice your chipping, always have a selection of clubs by your side as well as a batch of balls. By varying your shots you'll learn so much more quickly about touch and feel, the keys to a tidy short game. Don't just stand and hit the same chip one after the other. That's not nearly as meaningful.

2: Don't let tuition destroy your natural rhythm

DIAGNOSIS: As a teacher I'm forever conscious of the fact that tuition must never get in the way of the natural rhythm in a golfer's swing. I remember teaching Seve at Wentworth in 1979 and thinking: "I've got to be careful here." He had such a wonderful rhythm that I didn't want to tell him anything about his swing that might upset it. So all of my advice to him was in consideration of that fact.

EXPLANATION: When Seve was playing well there wasn't an ounce of tension in his body. The softness in his hands and arms was the oil that kept his swing running so smoothly. I believe that some of Seve's problems in the 1990s stem from the fact that he's become perhaps overly-concerned with techniques and swing thoughts,

which has never quite been his style, and has thus taken away some of that natural softness and impeded the free-flowing motion of his swing.

CORRECTION: This is a danger to any golfer. Whenever you get taught something new, the first instinct is to tighten-up and that process usually starts with the grip. You must be aware of this and avoid tension creeping into your hands and never lose the gift of being able to swing the club freely. Keeping your grip soft will almost certainly help. As Peter Thomson used to say: "Always grip lightly because you'll instinctively firm up at impact anyway." That's not a bad philosophy to bear in mind whenever you're trying to make changes in your swing.

In his prime Seve's swing had not an ounce of tension and such wonderful rhythm. Whenever a golfer is working on their game, perhaps making some swing changes, it's easy to lose this freedom, so be mindful of that when you're trying something new.

James Braid

This powerful and popular Scotsman had to travel south of the border to make a name for himself. Already a fine player, Braid's impressive fightback to square a 36-hole challenge match with multiple-Open champion JH Taylor gave him the confidence to go on to greater things, but also alerted the golfing world to a new pretender.

Harry Busson, an old golfing friend of mine who became a wonderful clubmaker, used to tell me all about James Braid so as a youngster I can remember having a good idea of what type of person he was and how he played the game. Born just a few miles along the coast from St Andrews, Braid would have had a jolly difficult job not at least discovering the game of golf. However, it would have been tough pursuing his love for the game. In the late 19th century golf professionals did not enjoy a particularly glorious social status and there certainly wasn't a lot of money in the game. Although Braid would have known from an early age that he had a talent for golf, juggling his time between a job as a joiner and an aspiring champion golfer would not have been easy.

Braid was one of the Great Triumvirate, alongside JH Taylor and Harry Vardon, and although Braid was marginally the eldest of the three – all born within 12 months of one another – he was the last to fulfil his enormous potential. Taylor was the young prodigy, if you like, winning a brace of Open titles before the other two had even opened their accounts. Vardon was the next to taste success, bristling with confidence as he claimed three Open victories in four years from 1896–1899. During the six or seven years that Taylor and Vardon were making off with the silverware, Braid was still busy trying to establish himself as a major force. Of course, he was already a fine player. But in championship terms he was what you might call a late developer, certainly in

comparison to his two great rivals. He endured some agonizing near-misses – most notably missing a putt to lose the Open to the brilliant amateur Harold Hilton at Hoylake in 1897 – and was thus doing an admirable job of perpetuating the theory that you had to lose a championship in order to learn how to win one.

But if Braid could be accused of being a slow learner, he sure had a good memory, because when he eventually acquired the knack of winning there was no stopping him. Indeed, despite giving his two great rivals a head-start of three championships apiece, Braid sprinted past Taylor and Vardon to become the first man to bag five victories in the Open Championship – and he did it all in the space of 10 years. No golfer other than Tom Watson has won more Opens in less time.

Braid also displayed a good sense of timing in securing a plum job as the first club pro at Walton Heath in Surrey. His success on the golf course had not changed him off it and he was very popular, known as much for his genial, larger-than-life character as he was for that famous, trademark bushy moustache that he sported in various shades from dark brown, to grey and silver. If time was harsh on the colour of his hair, it was gentler on his golf game and the skills that brought him five Open Championships stayed remarkably intact as the years went by. Indeed, he often beat his age by as much as 10 shots during the later years of his life.

Braid's prowess as a golf course architect was almost a match for his skills with a club and his name was in great demand throughout his non-competitive years. His expert eyes were the vision for one of this country's finest courses – the wonderful King's course at Gleneagles. Like the other two members of the Great Triumvirate, he succeeded in making his mark on the game in so many ways.

I find it incredible that these three men, all from poorish backgrounds, grew up to become such wonderful golfers, influential characters and perfect gentlemen. They played the game very differently, but they all conducted themselves impeccably. It was a shame that their playing careers were effectively cut short by the First World War, because when championship golf resumed in 1920 they were past their dominant best. The reign of the Great Triumvirate was over. A new era had dawned. It was time for Hagen, Sarazen and Jones to take centre stage.

3: Feel and imagination – a formidable combination

DIAGNOSIS: James Braid was a powerful, big-hitting player. He had a huge golf swing, well-oiled with lovely rhythm. He could be a little wild at times, but he had a wonderful short game to bail him out of trouble. You could say he was the recovery-play genius of his day, like an old-fashioned Seve Ballesteros or Arnold Palmer. He was that sort of player. Braid's strength was his strength, he could whack it out of anything – heather, deep rough, nothing was too thick for him. He'd simply use his brute force to shift mountains of turf, heather and soil and with that the ball would emerge, invariably landing on the desired part of the fairway or the green. Mind you any wayward golfer playing most of his golf around Walton Heath, where the heather bordering the fairways is terribly penal, would need to develop a bit of strength and a good short game or else be resigned to shooting high scores.

EXPLANATION: So, Braid had the touch, feel and imagination of a good player and the strength to go with it. In any era that's a formidable combination. One thing we must not overlook, though, is that Braid had a wonderful temperament which enabled him to make the most of the talent he was given. That's always the mark of a real champion – the mind allowing the body to perform to the absolute pinnacle of its ability. There are a thousand-and-one great ball-strikers for every champion golfer – all that separates them is the six inches between the ears.

Braid could be wild off the tee at times, most of golf's really big hitters are. But he had a fantastic temperament and a wonderful short game – two qualities that more than made up for the occasional missed fairway. And you don't win five Open Championships without being a great putter.

CORRECTION: So what can we learn from Braid's golf game. We know that his greatest weapons were his strength, combined with superb touch, feel and imagination. Well, these are all skills that we can enhance within our own games.

Strength is something you are either born with or can acquire through the appropriate training. If I were to recommend two key areas to develop physically for the benefit of your game they would definitely be the legs, along with the hands, wrists and forearms. Luckily, they are among the easiest parts of the body to build up.

The touch, feel and imagination of a brilliant short game are a combination of body and mind and with the right training these skills will develop hand in hand. It comes down to the way you see your short game. Don't assume one shot fits all situations – it doesn't. Even before you get to the ball you need to picture that shot in your mind, conjure up an image of the ball on its way to the hole, how it will react on the green. When you get to the ball, what options does the lie give you? If it's sitting well, you've all the choices in the world. If it's not, try to predict what sort of effect the lie will have on the spin and trajectory. When you decide on the shot, match the club that best performs that function – high or low, no run or lots of run. Now you can think about technique. Above all don't be afraid to experiment with shots – trial and error is one of golf's great teachers. And although it is wise to choose a club which best suits the

situation on the golf course, practicing with one club does wonders for developing the necessary touch and feel for this all-important department of the game.

As for having a champion's temperament, the Great Triumvirate possessed this quality in abundance and that is why to this day we still marvel at the achievements of James Braid, Harry Vardon and JH Taylor.

James Braid was an immensely strong player. Even when he found trouble off the tee he could whack it out of anything and had an uncanny ability to get it up and down in two from the most unlikely places. In that sense you could say he was much like Seve Ballesteros and Arnold Palmer.

Henry Cotton

Henry Cotton, my boyhood hero, was considered so great that Dunlop named a golf ball in commemoration of one of his rounds – a stunning 65 in the 1934 Open Championship at Sandwich. That was by three shots the lowest round of the tournament and it just about summed up Henry in his heyday – a class apart.

When I was a boy, Henry Cotton was the player of the moment. So when in 1938 my mother took me to the Open at Sandwich, I headed straight out to the practice ground to seek out my hero. My first sight of him was hitting shots with just his left arm. Even though I was only a boy I can remember how impressed I was. There was such wonderful rhythm in his swing and such crispness in the strike. Seeing Henry play was one of the best things that could have happened to me as a young golfer. It inspired me and also instilled in me the importance of rhythm.

When Henry started to hit full shots for real, he certainly showed the ball who was boss. I could actually hear his left heel thump down on the hard ground as he started his downswing. He collected himself so well in the downswing – every moving part was pouring down towards impact in one combined surge, there was not an ounce of wasted energy. Then, Boom! The strike, applied with such crushing authority.

Sitting here, some 60 or so years later, there's no doubt in my mind that in terms of ball-striking Henry was in the top-half-a-dozen of all time. I watched him play hundreds of times, but one particular moment stands out. It was during a matchplay event at Moortown in Yorkshire, in the late 1940s. He was playing against John Fallon, a good friend of mine whom I later played with in the Ryder Cup. They were both hitting their drives about the same distance off the tee, until they got to the par-five 10th hole where Henry hit it at least 50 yards past John. He had it in him all along, as do so many of the truly great players, but he'd kept that extra power in reserve until he

felt he really needed it. I spotted what Henry had done – he'd released the club earlier to create a wider downswing arc, almost slinging the clubhead at the ball and striking it more on the upswing. It went on forever. Poor John must have wondered what had hit him. I'm sure the golf ball did!

As a professional golfer myself, I got to know the man behind the legend. To be honest, you couldn't get close to Henry in the sense of being ever-so friendly with him. He didn't really mix with the other pros and was, I have to say, aloof and in some ways rather intimidating. But I never stopped admiring him tremendously for his golf. He was the best player, really a class apart. There were a lot of good players around at the time, but he was distinctly the best, no question. Perhaps his only slight weakness – and I'm talking very slight – was his bunker play. Relative to the rest of his game it was quite poor, but then again he was such a great player that he didn't get the chance to play many shots out of bunkers. Henry really was that good.

He'd always been a very dedicated player – and single-minded, too. Barely into his twenties he spurned the safety net of life as a club pro and set off to America with one ambition – to be the best player in the world, simple as that. Strangely enough, as we will soon discuss, he picked up a few bad swing traits in America. But in other ways, physically and perhaps more so mentally, it was the making of him as a golfer.

Soon afterwards he would put together a run of nine consecutive top-10 finishes in the Open Championship. Sadly for him, the Second World War robbed him of some of his best years, just as the First World War had interrupted the careers of the Great Triumvirate about 20 years earlier. Henry still captured three Open titles, including the memorable win at Sandwich in 1934 where he carried an amazing 10-shot lead into the final round, but I can't help thinking that given the opportunity he would have won more.

In a strange twist of fate, I found myself up against my boyhood hero in the final of the 1954 Penfold Matchplay tournament. I must be honest, he was still my hero even then – not the ideal frame of mind for a match! I'd been putting well and playing well all that week. The

final was played in pouring rain and it was blowing a gale. Dai Rees asked me if I would be interested in splitting the combined winner and runner-up purse. I told Dai: "If Henry agreed, I certainly would", since Henry was still someone I felt I was not in the same class as, even though he was then coming to the end of his career. I couldn't have been more surprised when Henry agreed. The trouble was as soon as I knew that I relaxed, which I believe may well have contributed to my being soundly beaten 5&4. That was a shame.

It's amazing when I think what that starry-eyed 14-year-old boy at the 1938 Open Championship would have thought had he known his hero would one day agree to share with him his prize money. Funny really. Life certainly can throw up a few surprises.

4: 'Collect yourself' and hit the ball on time

DIAGNOSIS: When it came to the golf swing, Henry used to always talk about the importance of the hands. Many of you reading this may even remember his trademark, hitting-a-tyre practice drill which he recommended for building up strength in the hands and wrists.

However, in all this talk about the hands one factor got overlooked – namely, Henry's immensely strong legs. They were like tree trunks, providing a stable base for his swing and supporting a wonderful body action that was always perfectly in tune with his hands and arms.

And therein lies the real key. As I described earlier, Henry collected himself as he started his downswing in such a way that culminated in all the moving parts surging towards the ball as one, and arriving at impact together. No moving part worked independently of another in Henry's downswing and the result was a strike of awesome authority.

EXPLANATION: It wasn't always like that. As a youngster Henry was a very straight hitter who played with a relatively weak left-hand grip. When he went to America in 1929 and discovered that everyone was playing with a strong grip and hitting a draw in the search for extra length, he changed his whole style of play in order to draw the ball also. He took the club back way on the inside in the takeaway, then lifted the club quite abruptly to the top of his backswing – not unlike Sandy Lyle. Unlike Sandy, however, Henry then swung down into impact very much from the inside and hit all of his shots with a big hook. That almost cost him the Open in 1934, because the wind really blew on the last day and he couldn't hold the ball up. It kept running away from him. His swing wasn't as mechanically sound then as it later became. He soon realized it wasn't right and worked hard at reverting to a neutral grip, so that his clubface was more open, allowing him to release the club freely without fear of the big hook.

Henry had strong hands and arms but it was the timing of his downswing which generated such devastating power – every moving part surging towards impact and arriving together to deliver a crushing blow to the back of the ball.

CORRECTION: The co-ordination in Henry's downswing – call it harmony of movement if you like – is a wonderful lesson for us all. You don't want to be all legs and no hands and arms in the downswing, which is what much of golf instruction in the sixties, seventies and eighties advocated. Equally you don't want all hands and arms and no leg action. There needs to be a balance – the body unwinding at the same time as the hands and arms swing the club down. You should feel that as you start your downswing you collect together all the moving parts of your swing and that they arrive simultaneously at impact.

Another related point worth stressing is not to be obsessed with this mythical 'late hit'. This has been way over-emphasized for many years, to the extent that I would say that during my career 90 per cent of club golfers hit too late. By that, I mean the wrists are cocked for way too long in the downswing which makes it impossible to release the clubhead at speed into the back of the ball. Some pupils have even come to me and said: "John I want to learn how to hit late." I usually reply: "What's wrong with hitting it at the right time?" So, rather than trying to hit late, you would be better off thinking of free-wheeling the club into and through impact. That kind of mental imagery encourages you to release the angles in your wrists at the right time in the downswing, which enables you to hit the back of the ball on time!

Many club golfers are obsessed with the so-called late-hit, but would be much better off thinking in terms of free-wheeling the clubhead into the back of the ball. This encourages you to release the angles in your wrists at exactly the right moment in the swing – that's what great timing is all about and it's amazing what a difference that makes to the quality of your ball-striking.

Ben Crenshaw

Softly spoken, likeable and charming – Ben Crenshaw fits all of these descriptions. Until, that is, he steps on to any putting green at which point he becomes a ruthless marksman, his trusty putter the deadliest and most accurate of weapons.

Ever since Young Tom Morris followed in the hob-nailed footsteps of his white-bearded father Old Tom, talented young golfers have had to endure comparisons with their illustrious forebears and therefore shoulder the expectations of a public anxiously looking for their next hero. When I was growing up, every teenage star was eyed as the possible 'next Bobby Jones'. Many years later, Ben Hogan became the 'next' best thing. Then it was Arnold Palmer. It's funny, but gifted young golfers hardly ever seem to be the first of a new kind, they are always the next of a previous kind.

Ben Crenshaw will have known what this felt like. He was an outstanding amateur who had the dubious pleasure of being labelled the 'next Jack Nicklaus'. Many more young golfers would subsequently be conferred the same 'honour' and while I'm sure the comparisons are initially flattering, it's a heavy burden of expectation to dump on the shoulders of any young man. Mind you, Ben coped better than many others. In 1973, as a 21-year-old, he entered the tour school and won it by 12 shots. He then won the first event he played in as a professional, the 1974 Texas Open, and the following week finished second.

The problem with sprinting out of the blocks this quickly is that people expect you to break the world record. In golfing terms that could mean only one thing – Ben had to win a major. In the years that followed I noticed how Ben frequently got into a position to challenge, but couldn't quite summon the decisive blow. Two years in succession he finished runner-up in the Open Championship, once ironically to Jack Nicklaus, and either side of that he was third and fifth. Ben was also second in the Masters twice and sandwiched in-between that he lost a sudden death playoff to David Graham for the 1979 USPGA. It was this frustrating sequence of near misses that led to Ben developing a reputation as the 'nearly man' – a time when no doubt he longed for those halcyon days when he was dubbed the next Jack Nicklaus!

Although some might disagree, I don't think Ben was ever a choker. In my view it boiled down to the simple fact that his long and elegant swing, blessed with wonderful rhythm, wasn't quite as good as it looked. His body pivot wasn't quite right, which is what most long swingers suffer from, and that caused his hands and arms to work independently at the top of his backswing letting the club travel too far. When he developed a better body turn, the arms swung more in sympathy with that turn and he managed to shorten his swing and became a much more consistent player.

But in the final analysis, that isn't why Ben eventually won a major. No, he made the breakthrough because he managed to get his putter working when it really mattered – Sunday afternoon. I recently watched a video tape of his first Masters win in 1984 and I'd forgotten just how many putts he holed. It was one of the most astonishing putting performances I've ever seen. The same thing happened again when he won in 1995, although the sheer yardage of holed putts was no match for his first triumph 11 years earlier. This time around I thought Davis Love had that tournament in the bag, but on the back nine Ben's putter suddenly woke up and he holed a succession of great putts, none better than a wickedly curling 15-footer on the 17th. "The prettiest putt I ever hit" was how he later described it. Almost before you could work out what was going on, Ben was strolling up the hill on the 18th with a two-shot lead.

It was one of those victories that you look back on and think, "well, that was meant to be." Only days before the tournament started Ben had been the pallbearer at Harvey Penick's funeral. Harvey had been Ben's coach from boyhood, not so much in the style of a swing guru but rather a confidant who's wisdom and experience helped guide Ben throughout his professional career. That week at Augusta, Ben said he still felt influenced by Harvey's presence, almost like he had "a 15th club in my bag."

It was definitely one of the most emotional finales to any tournament I've seen. Ben did well to hold it all in, but as soon as the job was done and the final putt fell, he broke down in tears. A very poignant moment.

There have been lots of better players than Ben this century, but there really hasn't been a better putter. On top of all that he's a very nice guy, the sort of man who you imagine would never say a bad word about anyone. There's obviously some justice left in the world because I've never heard anyone say a bad word about Ben, either.

5: The correct impact factors

DIAGNOSIS: Ben has a very distinctive putting stroke. He stands very tall, his arms relatively straight, and from there he pivots his body. His arms and the putter move directly in harmony with that pivot. There are no abrupt movements, the putter changes direction very smoothly and accelerates gradually as it strikes the ball. It's all very much one-piece, with no independent hand and wrist action. The actual path of the putter is back and through on the inside, but then 'square-through' at impact, popping the ball towards the hole with piston-like accuracy.

EXPLANATION: Ben himself has said that: "I try to build my putts around pace" and an inside-to-square method is great for achieving this because it encourages the putter to swing freely. When I was a boy I practiced my putting until my back hurt and all along I remember trying to get the putter to swing back and forth in a dead-straight line. It was only when I watched Arnold Palmer and Gary Player putt and noticed that the putter went back on the inside and through square to the line of the putt, that I realized the error of my ways. Ben's method involves an exaggerated in-to-square path and, as I say, I like the way it gets the putter swinging freely through the ball. The essence of Ben's success, though, is that he manages to get the putter swinging through the ball along the correct line, with the putter-face

Ben's putting stroke involves a distinctly inside-the-line backswing, from where he manages to produce the perfect impact factors – the putter swinging through on-line with the putter-face exactly square to that line.

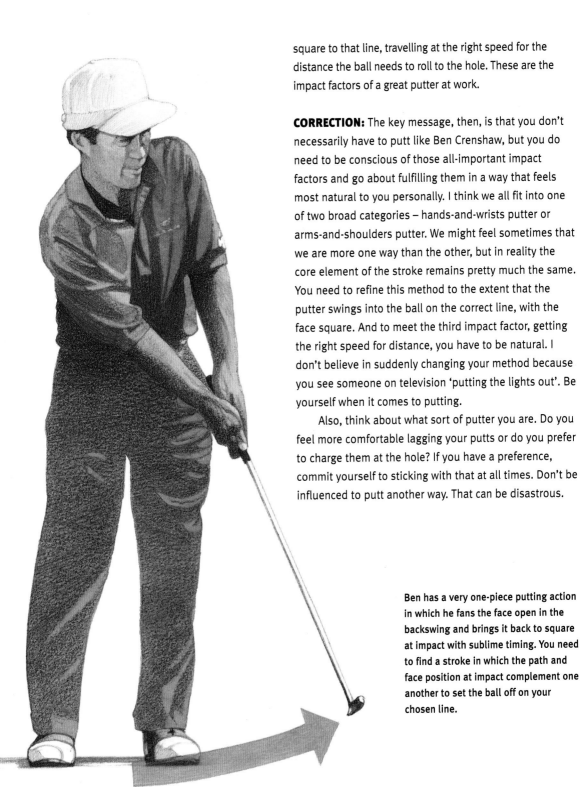

square to that line, travelling at the right speed for the distance the ball needs to roll to the hole. These are the impact factors of a great putter at work.

CORRECTION: The key message, then, is that you don't necessarily have to putt like Ben Crenshaw, but you do need to be conscious of those all-important impact factors and go about fulfilling them in a way that feels most natural to you personally. I think we all fit into one of two broad categories – hands-and-wrists putter or arms-and-shoulders putter. We might feel sometimes that we are more one way than the other, but in reality the core element of the stroke remains pretty much the same. You need to refine this method to the extent that the putter swings into the ball on the correct line, with the face square. And to meet the third impact factor, getting the right speed for distance, you have to be natural. I don't believe in suddenly changing your method because you see someone on television 'putting the lights out'. Be yourself when it comes to putting.

Also, think about what sort of putter you are. Do you feel more comfortable lagging your putts or do you prefer to charge them at the hole? If you have a preference, commit yourself to sticking with that at all times. Don't be influenced to putt another way. That can be disastrous.

Ben has a very one-piece putting action in which he fans the face open in the backswing and brings it back to square at impact with sublime timing. You need to find a stroke in which the path and face position at impact complement one another to set the ball off on your chosen line.

Ernie Els

A smooth rhythm and a laid-back image; the power to effortlessly launch 300-yard drives, combined with a sweet short game – no wonder Ernie Els is a joy to watch. It also explains why this big man is one of a small group of golfers earmarked to dominate the game in the 21st century.

Mention the name Ernie Els and superlatives flow like the swing of the man himself. Seve said he was "a golfer from another planet." Hale Irwin said "he is no overnight sensation. He is a truly great player." Gary Player said "when I first saw Ernie play golf, I knew I was witnessing one of the next generation of superstars." That's a lot of praise for one man, but it was indicative of the fuss this big South African caused when the spotlight first fell on his burly frame. I remember in the early 1990s talking to Laddy Lucas, who'd seen just about every great golfer of the 20th century, who said of Ernie: "There's one that'll go all the way to the top."

I couldn't wait to get a close look at Ernie in action and when I watched him during the PGA Championship at Wentworth in 1994 I wasn't disappointed. Even just hitting balls on the range you could tell he was a class act. But it's out on the course where he really separates himself from the crowd. Let me put it like this: I would say there are three types of tour player. There is the journeyman pro who plays consistent if unspectacular golf and earns a good living, maybe even winning the occasional tournament. There is the top-class golfer who wins several tournaments, becoming rich without ever really setting the world on fire. Then there is a third category – golf's minority group, the world beaters. These are the players who burst on to the scene at a young age, win a hatful of tournaments at the blink of an eye and go on to win majors – usually several. Ben Hogan, Sam Snead, Arnold Palmer, Gary Player, Byron Nelson, Henry Cotton, Jack Nicklaus,

Seve Ballesteros and Nick Faldo – these are the type of golfers who fit into this group. In my opinion, so does Ernie Els. He has all the necessary ingredients of the model major-winner. He has a brilliant all round game with no apparent deficiencies. "My weaknesses aren't far behind all of my strengths," is how he describes himself, a typically modest statement from Ernie.

Above all, he has a great attitude and temperament for the big occasion – the owner of an unflappable set of feathers that you would be hard-pressed to ruffle. For evidence, look no further than the shot he hit into the penultimate hole of the 1997 US Open. The way he drew in that five-iron, to a flag positioned back-left with water down the left side and beyond the green, was simply awesome. One of the most courageous shots I've ever seen. That coolness under pressure, to hit the big shots at the big moments, is what I believe will enable Ernie to win many majors in the next millennium.

The talent has been there for a long time. Despite saying he was 'useless' (his word, not mine) when he first started playing golf, he was down to scratch by the time he was 14 and World Junior champion a year later. When he turned pro at 19 he made an immediate and sizeable impression, entirely in keeping with his imposing physique. He was the first man since Gary Player to win a hat-trick of the South African PGA, the South African Masters and the South African Open titles. More significantly, he showed signs of a definite major championship pedigree. In his first two Opens as a professional he finished fifth and sixth, and at Sandwich in 1993 he was the first man in history to break 70 in all four rounds of an Open. In the 1994 US Open he didn't merely get into contention to win, he did win, with a mature and impressive mixture of brilliance and resilience on one of the most fearsome courses in America, Oakmont.

To come out as a youngster and perform so well, so soon, at the highest level shows real class. His prolific strike rate around the world since then merely confirms what many said about him, that he is a truly great player. Even when he's not at his best he can win tournaments,

another sign of the finest pedigree, and besides, I always get the feeling with golfers like Ernie that a return to top form is just one good swing away.

There's no doubt that when the cavalry of great young golfers rides into the next millennium, Ernie will be one of those leading the charge. Although knowing what Ernie's like it won't be so much of a charge, more that unhurried yet somehow purposeful amble of his. 'Don't hurry and don't worry' seems to be Ernie's philosophy to golf. That kind of attitude will take him far.

6: Find a way to turn

DIAGNOSIS: Ernie's golf swing is very much the finished article. He flows through positions with a fluidity and grace that few come close to matching. It has no idiosyncrasies, no wasted energy or unnecessary movement. It's efficient and tremendously powerful, with a full and correct use of the body, yet it is in no way mechanical. Indeed, there's lots of freedom in his swing. It's wonderful to watch.

EXPLANATION: In my opinion he plays golf in the way that would be best pictured in the minds of everyone reading this book, except those who suffer from a bad hook, and that is swinging the club from in-to-in, producing a slight draw. Tom Watson plays the game just the same. In some ways you could compare the action to a footballer hitting an inswinging corner, the boot approaching the ball from the inside imparting the sidespin that creates the right-to-left ball flight. The physics are the same in golf, the clubhead swinging into the ball from inside the target line, creating sidespin to make the ball draw. All this is possible because Ernie makes the perfect turn, with just the correct amount of tilt brought about by the perfect posture. I'm sure he can fade the ball when necessary, but for the most part he lets it fly, eschewing the safe shot.

CORRECTION: Ernie achieves this massive upper-body turn without lifting his left heel. The hips don't turn much, either, so together that creates lots of resistance in the legs – the action of a supple man and a powerful hitter. Most of you reading this will not be as supple as Ernie, but it's important that you find a way to turn your body however is appropriate for you personally. For many, this means making certain compromises, such as lifting the left heel to 'release' the left side and thus make it possible to turn. You won't generate as much resistance in the legs, but it's better to do that than keep your left heel planted which might not give you the flexibility to make a sufficient turn.

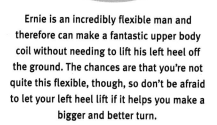

Ernie is an incredibly flexible man and therefore can make a fantastic upper body coil without needing to lift his left heel off the ground. The chances are that you're not quite this flexible, though, so don't be afraid to let your left heel lift if it helps you make a bigger and better turn.

7: GASPing for a better golf swing

Ernie's fundamentals are flawless, impressive for a big man, and much of what is great about his golf swing can be attributed to this wonderful address position. You, too, will benefit from a better golf swing if you pay more attention to the fundamentals at address.

Adopting a waggle at address (far right) will help you keep tension out of your hands.

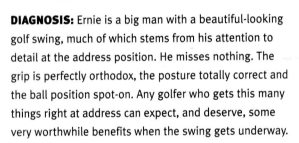

DIAGNOSIS: Ernie is a big man with a beautiful-looking golf swing, much of which stems from his attention to detail at the address position. He misses nothing. The grip is perfectly orthodox, the posture totally correct and the ball position spot-on. Any golfer who gets this many things right at address can expect, and deserve, some very worthwhile benefits when the swing gets underway.

EXPLANATION: This attention to detail is lost on most club golfers – they assume someone as good as Ernie works on fancy swing theories all the time. Not so. He works on his fundamentals just like any other golfer should. In my experience, it is the club golfers who are least likely to work on these basics when ironically it is they who need to most. Over the years I've been forever reminding pupils to check their grip, aim, stance and posture – GASP. And I'm going to do it again now.

CORRECTION: The grip must make it possible to control the clubface for the individual. The aim of the clubface

fixes the ball position and therefore the stance. Correct posture makes possible the correct body turn which creates the necessary in-to-in arc so vital in order to release the club at speed through the hitting area.

One final thing. Take a leaf out of Ernie's book and develop a pre-swing waggle. It's the simplest of movements. Just move the club away from the ball and back again by softly hingeing your wrists back and forth. A couple of those is enough and it just stops you gripping the club too tightly and thus prevents tension creeping into your hands and arms. So when your swing does get underway, the first move away is more likely to be a smooth one. That should do wonders for the rhythm of your swing.

29

Nick Faldo

As a young boy Nick Faldo dismantled a perfectly decent bike in order to find out exactly how it worked. Many years later he did the very same thing to his golf swing and put it back together to become the most successful British golfer of the 20th century.

Through his association with David Leadbetter, his single minded approach and sheer capacity for hard work on his swing, Nick Faldo has I believe been unfairly labelled a somewhat mechanical, almost manufactured, golfer. That doesn't do justice to his remarkable talent, so perhaps now is as good a time as any to dispel these misconceptions. Consider this – he started playing golf when he was 14 and within four years won the English Amateur Championship and the British Youths, along with eight (yes, eight) other amateur titles in a 10-month winning spree. Two years later he won the PGA

Championship, Europe's most prestigious tournament behind the Open, and later that year in his first Ryder Cup singles beat the reigning US Masters and Open champion Tom Watson. By 1983 his stroke average had plummeted to just about bang-on 69, the lowest of any golfer in the world that year, and he topped the European Money List for the first time. Manufactured? Mechanical? I don't think so.

Despite the success, Nick knew he could do better and I suspect his painful back-nine collapse in the 1983 Open, when he had a sniff of victory, merely hammered that point home even more forcibly. "I've been close in a couple of Opens and not been able to finish the job," he said at the time. "The problem is my

technique – or lack of it." When he then joined forces with David Leadbetter, in my opinion they started working on exactly the right things straight away. Everyone questioned whether he was doing the right thing but I felt sure he was and wrote quoting the names of players who had gone from "good to great" by changing their swings. I know it's easy for me to say this with the benefit of hindsight, but I promise you it's exactly how I felt at the time. It was a courageous decision of Nick's, but absolutely the correct one.

I strongly believe that he'd have struggled to win a single major, let alone six, with the swing he had then. Yes, he was a marvellous player when he was in the groove. But his action relied enormously on a good hand action and perfect rhythm and timing. The core elements of his swing, namely the body and leg action, were simply not good enough. I remember the second time I was captain of the Ryder Cup team, at Walton Heath in 1981. In the initial player meeting I made a point of saying, as I had in 1979: "You wouldn't be in the team if you weren't good players, so I'm not about to start teaching anyone this week." At the end of the morning matches on the second day Nick said to me: "Don't pick me this afternoon, I can't hit my hat." His already upright swing had become so straight that he either dropped the club on the inside coming down and hit a push or came way over the top and pull-hooked it. Not even his great short game – and people forget just how good a putter he was in the late seventies and early eighties – could save him. I said to Nick: "I'm going to break my rule, let's meet on the practice ground first thing tomorrow for a lesson." We had

a good session the next morning and I used the arc of his swing to get the body out of the way, making room for his hands and arms to swing the club down and through on the correct path. He went out in the afternoon and beat Johnny Miller 2&1.

By the late eighties and early nineties you'd have had a tough time convincing me that he wasn't the best player in the world. Six major championships in less than a decade is a fantastic strike rate. He's also won more Ryder Cup matches than any other player in history. I've always been impressed with Nick's single-minded and dedicated approach to his golf. This work ethic and unflinching desire for perfection enabled him to make the

absolute most of the enormous talent he showed as a youngster – nothing, as far as Nick was concerned, would get in the way of his goals.

When his teacher at school told him that only one in a thousand golfers were successful, it spurred him on even more. When he felt his swing was holding him back, he restructured it and made it better. And when he was the best player in the world, he strived for perfection in the way Ben Hogan had 50 years previously. Nick wanted to control the ball like it was on a piece of string. People today say, 'Did you see Ben Hogan play golf?' And I know in years to come Nick would like people to ask the same question of him. They may well.

8: Don't forget your hands

DIAGNOSIS: Nick was brought up in the Jack Nicklaus era of technique, swinging too straight with the body tilting in the backswing. Effectively, his body action and arm-swing were on the same plane which was too steep. Now, if you swing too straight and the body gets out of the way in the downswing, you hit the biggest pull-hooks imaginable. So to counter that you develop a lateral hip slide, characterized by the pronounced leg action that you used to see in Nick's game.

EXPLANATION: Nick's swing changes centred around a few key elements of his swing. He widened his stance a little so that his legs would stabilize and support a more rotary body action. He then focused on winding his body over a more passive leg and hip action, which created resistance – in effect, energy – that he would then use to drive a more powerful downswing. The arms swung in response to the body motion, whereas in his swing of old the hands and arms dominated the action and the body went along for the ride. Basically, Nick went from being a very handsy player to a more body-controlled, passive-hands player.

CORRECTION: That was just the ticket for Nick, but over-emphasis on body action is dangerous territory for the average golfer because it assumes you have a great hand action and to be frank, most club golfers suffer from a lack of hand action rather than too much. That's why I often prefer to use the arc of the swing to get the body moving. This medicine will be good for your swing if you tend to hit the ball very high, often hitting a push with a left-to-right shape, mixed with the occasional snap hook. Once you get the correct in-to-in picture of the swing path, your body will clear out of the way virtually automatically and thus you won't need to drive the legs to avoid coming over the top. The correct in-back-to-in arc creates the proper release of the hands and thus the clubhead through the ball.

In his early twenties Nick was a very fine player, but his swing was essentially too straight and too reliant on a perfectly-timed hand action.

After a complete makeover his posture improved and the shape of his swing became much more rotary.

9: Soft hands give your chipping more feel

DIAGNOSIS: Nick has often been accused of being mechanical, but I don't agree. Certainly not when you look at the way he plays little chip shots and pitches, where I think there's great fluidity and softness to his technique.

EXPLANATION: That's because although Nick is a very strong, muscular individual, he has wonderful touch. For a start he has a great looking grip, which he applies to the club with just the right amount of pressure. A soft, but secure hold. And although I know Nick then likes to feel that the trunk of his body controls the motion of his swing, his hands and arms stay so soft that the club flows back and forth ever so smoothly and very correctly. It looks, feels and is extremely controlled.

CORRECTION: When you practice your chipping, try to adopt a posture whereby the hands and arms hang free from tension and keep your grip nice and soft. Then, as you swing the club back with your arms and shoulders, feel a little bit of 'give' in your wrists as the club changes direction from backswing to downswing. That 'lag' effect is exactly what you want and is created by the shoulders unwinding through the ball. It establishes the correct angles in your wrists and helps to make sure your hands lead the club into impact. The clubhead will meet the ball on the ideal angle of attack – striking it sweetly but still with a sense of authority. No sloppiness, no mis-hits, just perfect ball-turf contact. And the great thing is you can apply that technique to any club from a six-iron to a sandwedge to produce a whole range of shots.

Ideal posture frees the arms of tension. The hands, arms and shoulders then stay very connected, a soft grip pressure allowing the wrists to flex just the right amount as Nick changes direction from backswing to downswing, resulting in a very crisp strike. You can't go far wrong if you introduce these fine qualities into your own chipping action.

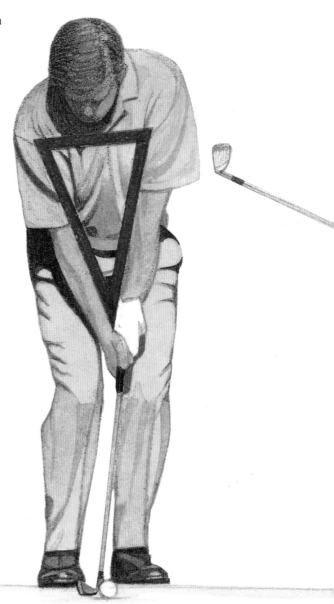

Ray Floyd

Golf at the highest level is a game for hard men – and they don't come any harder than Ray Floyd. He had a look that could wither opponents at 50 paces and next to Jack Nicklaus had probably the best temperament of any player over the last half a century. One might say his golf swing was no oil painting, but it produced strokes worthy of any masterpiece.

Meet the golfer once dubbed by his fellow tour pros as 'the toughest man on Tuesdays' for his reputation as a ferocious competitor before the serious business of tournament play had even started. The thing was, Ray always found practice rounds pretty mundane affairs so he would spice them up a bit by placing some hard cash on the line. "Playing for your own money is a great way to learn how to compete under the heat," he once said. The fact he could afford to lose was irrelevant – he didn't want to lose and that brought out the competitive best in him.

This hard school of learning was Ray's education in the game. He'd grown up gambling on the golf course, the driving range, the putting green – anywhere you could hit a golf shot was a good enough place for a wager and he soon realized that his fortunes swung on the swing of a golf club. When he came out of the US Army and joined the professional tour, he soon developed a reputation as a serious hustler, frequently playing challenge matches for $1,000-plus a time. On one occasion he lost two consecutive games to a young pro called Lee Trevino, which cost him and his backers several thousand dollars. The backers wanted to cut their losses and leave town, but Ray insisted on another showdown and doubled the stakes, putting in $2,000 from his own back pocket. When he and Trevino butted heads again the next day, they came to the last hole dead level, but Ray holed a 20-foot eagle putt on the 18th green to shoot 63 and pip Trevino by a shot. On evidence like that it's little wonder Ray became one of golf's real hard men, as tough a competitor as you could ever dread to come up against.

In his twenties Ray could play just as hard off the golf course and, given the circumstances – a young bachelor with plenty of money in his back pocket – it is hardly surprising he found it so easy to have such a great time. But living the high life did nothing for his golf and for a few years he didn't do justice to his phenomenal talent. The love of a good woman seemed to put Ray back on the straight and narrow and wedded bliss did wonders for his golf game. He'd had success before, but not like this. In the 1976 Masters he opened with a 66, added a 65 the next day and strutted to an eight-shot victory, sharing a scoring record with Jack Nicklaus that would stand for 22 years. He also shared Nicklaus' coach, Jack Grout, and under the old man's guidance a steady flow of trophies found there way on to the Floyd mantelpiece and a flood of money poured into his bank account. He proved what a tremendously enduring competitor he was in the 1986 US Open when at the age of 43 he shot a cool and calculated final round of 66 at Shinnecock Hills to land his fourth and final major championship.

His tournament victories spanned four decades, as did his appearances in the Ryder Cup. He had turned 51 by the time he played in his final match at The Belfry in 1993 and in the singles beat Jose Maria Olazabal, a man just about half his age, in what he says was one of the best rounds of his life. Few could argue with that. Halfway into that match Ray realized how important his game would be to the final outcome and produced a four hole spell of inspired golf when he really needed it. That is a measure of the man. I only ever saw him once hit a bad shot under pressure, when from the perfect position in the middle of the fairway he put his eight-iron approach shot in the water on the second playoff hole against Nick Faldo at the 1990 Masters – and I couldn't have been more surprised. He was the last person in the world I would have expected to do that. But as always with Ray there were no histrionics. As he once said: "Golf is a gentlemen's game and I think you should expect to win or lose under the gentlemen's code."

Ray certainly did that, conducting himself impeccably while at the top of his game, just as Jack Nicklaus did for all those years. He has always been a charming man and I think irrespective of his record, which is so impressive, one of Ray Floyd's greatest achievements is that he would be a very good role model for any youngster. If his career hadn't run parallel with Jack Nicklaus', I think many would acknowledge his achievements with even greater acclaim.

10: Stand tall and let your arms hang when you putt

DIAGNOSIS: The first time I saw Ray Floyd play golf was during the 1969 Ryder Cup at Royal Birkdale. He had just turned 27 years of age and arrived in England fresh from winning the USPGA Championship, his first major victory. Back in those days he was swinging like most young American tour pros of that era, 'rocking and blocking' – in other words, too much emphasis on body tilt rather than the correct body turn, which caused the arms to swing on a very upright plane. The fact he had won a major with a distinctly unsound technique says a lot about Ray's talent, but he soon realized this wasn't the way forward and worked on turning his shoulders properly. The trouble was, the hands and arms still wanted to follow the shoulders' lead, which would have made his swing incredibly flat. That wouldn't do, either, so to avoid this Ray developed a method whereby the club would start back on the inside from where he swung the club up quite abruptly to get it into a good position at the top. The result has never been pretty to look at, but my word it always got the job done.

Ray was a very sound ball-striker but perhaps his greatest strength, other than a champion's temperament,

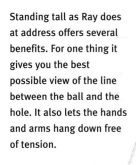

Standing tall as Ray does at address offers several benefits. For one thing it gives you the best possible view of the line between the ball and the hole. It also lets the hands and arms hang down free of tension.

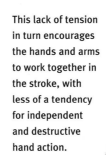

This lack of tension in turn encourages the hands and arms to work together in the stroke, with less of a tendency for independent and destructive hand action.

It also encourages a very free swing of the hands and arms, so the putter follows a smooth and most likely correct path back and forth enabling you to set the ball off on the chosen line more consistently.

has been his short game. He's a marvellous chipper and bunker player, also a wonderful putter with a distinctive style that you could recognize from a mile away. He uses a longer-than-standard putter and stands very tall, more upright than any other golfer I can think of, with his hands high. It is in most ways completely opposite to Jack Nicklaus, who tends to crouch over the ball with his arms very bent and tucked in close to his body. I say most ways, because the two methods share the characteristic of being highly effective.

EXPLANATION: The best way I can sum up Ray's putting stroke is to say that he swings his hands, as opposed to his hands swinging the putter. By that, I mean his hands swing on a consistent arc back and forth and the putter simply responds to that motion. That's a good way to putt. There is no need for manipulation of the putter mid-stroke and thus there is no independent hand action. You get the definite impression that everything is working together in Ray's stroke. Of all the different styles of putting that I explore in this book, that is perhaps the only single common denominator.

CORRECTION: As I see it there are three distinct benefits to Ray's style of putting. For one thing, standing tall gives you a very good view of the hole and indeed the line to the hole, and if you can see the line you can hit the line.

Secondly, an upright posture encourages the arms to hang down relatively free from tension. You don't want the arms ramrod straight, but instead flexed slightly with the elbows pointing in towards your body. This naturally comfortable position encourages the hands, arms and putter to operate as a team. There's less of a tendency for the hands and arms to 'fight' one another during the stroke.

Thirdly, as we've already touched upon, standing tall over the ball puts you in a super position to make a very free swing of the hands and arms which encourages the putter to track back and forth smoothly and more than likely on the correct path. Everything flows. There is no jerky or abrupt movement to upset the path of the putter.

So is Ray's method for you? Well, I always say to my pupils that if you don't have a problem holing putts, don't change a thing. But if you feel you don't hole enough short and medium length putts, give it a go.

A simple way to sum up Ray's putting stroke is that he swings his hands, as opposed to his hands swinging the putter, and the putter simply responds to that movement. Everything works in harmony, which is why it is such an effective method.

Walter Hagen

The great showman. Walter Hagen went through life like a Hollywood actor, but his golf was definitely no charade. Behind the flamboyant clothes, the fast cars and the adoring female entourage was a golfer of enormous talent who had a profound influence on the professional game.

I would love to have spent some time with Walter Hagen. Not because he was the best player, but because he was the most amazing character. Even the black-and-white photography of the day cannot disguise Hagen's colourful lifestyle. Here was a marvellous golfer who well and truly lived his life in the fast lane.

The stories about his career are as memorable as they are entertaining. I remember him winning Opens and giving his first prize to his caddie. Everywhere he went in the world – land or sea, Bentley or boat – he travelled first class. Nothing else would do. Hagen's capacity for socializing and having a great time was legendary – he probably drank more champagne than all the other golfers of his generation put together! They say he was probably the first golfer to make a million dollars, in which case he was definitely the first golfer to blow a million. Mind you, he always said he didn't want to be a millionaire, just live like one!

When this flamboyant New Yorker first came over to England for the 1920 Open Championship at Deal, he was staggered to find that as a professional golfer he wasn't allowed in the clubhouse. It was an act of snobbery that Hagen simply could not abide, so he responded by hiring a Daimler, a chauffeur to drive it and a footman to carry his belongings. He would pull up outside the clubhouse in the morning, change his shoes and walk on to the tee; then have the car and his personal attendants waiting behind the 18th green when he

finished his round. The man certainly had style.

Hagen burnt the candle at both ends, but it didn't seem to affect his golf. Technically he wasn't that special. His first love had been baseball and you could see a touch of this in his golf swing. That stance of his was unusually wide. And there was a tremendous amount of lateral movement, swaying off the ball quite dramatically in the backswing and almost lunging towards the target as he swung into and through impact. It lacked beauty, but it got the job done.

Besides, Hagen had a secret weapon up his sleeve – temperament. Mentally he was in a different class. When you consider that he won four USPGA Championships in a row, at a time when it was a matchplay event, that's simply incredible. I don't care how talented a golfer is, you can't play well every day. So to be unbeaten for four years, I would have to put that success down to Hagen's dominant character and confidence, as much as his golf game. In the Ryder Cup he was an awesome force to be reckoned with. He played in five teams and lost only once to the tenacious and talented Scot, George Duncan.

One of the other things I find amazing about Hagen is that he was able to combine a real champion's temperament and intense will to win with a genuinely laid-back character. He was famous for coining the phrase: "Never hurry, never worry, and be sure to smell the flowers along the way." This wasn't one of those glib platitudes that some people say for effect. Hagen meant it. Nothing worried him. He went out on the golf course fully expecting to hit several bad shots. So when the odd one came along, as they inevitably do to us all, Hagen shrugged it off and turned his attentions to the next shot.

It's funny really, because in some ways this devil-may-care, flamboyant image now disguises what a truly remarkable player he was. We are talking about one of the most prolific winners in the history of golf. He won nine major championships in the 1920s alone and his final tally of 11 professional majors – four Open Championships, two US Opens and five USPGAs – is second only to Jack Nicklaus. Let's not forget, either, that he had only three majors to play for. The US Masters

didn't even exist when Hagen was in his prime.

Laid-back, charismatic, cheerful, entertaining – Walter Hagen was all of these. But underneath the playful outward demeanour was a man with serious talent. I remember being told of an occasion where he played a golf course that was so hard and fast-running that it was impossible to stop the ball on the greens. So Hagen aimed his approach shots at the most conveniently-positioned bunker, safe in the knowledge that he could get it up and down for his par, no problem. Hagen was a showman, all right. But he had the skills and the brains to back up the bravado.

11: Keep your head down? Forget it!

DIAGNOSIS: Walter Hagen was a classic example of a great player with a lot of head movement in his swing. There have been many over the years, but he was perhaps the most conspicuous exponent. From a wide stance he dragged the club away, his whole upper body swaying to the right, from where he lunged towards the target in the downswing and on to his left side in the followthrough. This is infinitely preferable to staying completely still, with no weight transfer at all during the swing.

EXPLANATION: When I was on the instruction panel of the American magazine *Golf Digest* in the 1960s they carried out a survey of the leading 50 money winners on tour. They photographed each golfer hitting shots, with a grid-pattern positioned behind them so that it was possible to monitor their head movement during their swing. Of these, 48 of the 50 golfers moved their head to the right in the backswing. Some moved more than others and two golfers remained centred. But, not surprisingly since these were all good players, none moved to the left.

CORRECTION: This obsession among some golfers to keep the head down has kept me busy for 50 years. It's like strapping a straight jacket on to a golfer – it restricts a full, free turn, so essential for both power and accuracy. So if ever I hear of a golfer whose main swing thought is to keep their head down throughout the swing, the alarm bells ring in my head. In any good golf swing there is invariably a certain amount of lateral movement of the head and body. So long as this body action is harmonized with the hand and arm action, it is allowable and in many cases desirable for there to be a degree of lateral movement.

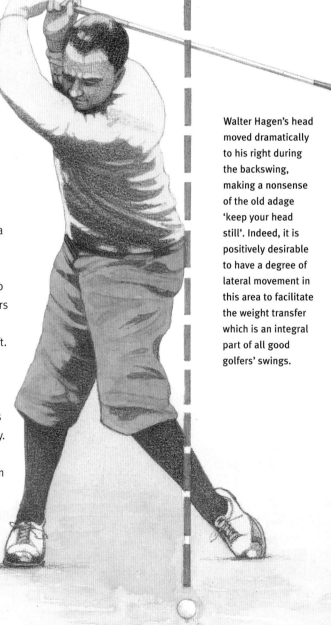

Walter Hagen's head moved dramatically to his right during the backswing, making a nonsense of the old adage 'keep your head still'. Indeed, it is positively desirable to have a degree of lateral movement in this area to facilitate the weight transfer which is an integral part of all good golfers' swings.

12: Attitude of the man maketh the golfer

DIAGNOSIS: Walter Hagen was truly the king of matchplay. Obviously he was no fool when it came to strokeplay, either, but somehow head-to-head combat brought out the best in him. Much of his success would have to be attributed to his totally unflappable nature. Bobby Jones, who suffered his worst ever defeat at the hands of Hagen, an 11&10 drubbing over four rounds, said that it was a joy to play with him. "He goes along chin up," Jones described, "smiling away, never grousing about his luck, playing the ball as he finds it."

EXPLANATION: This is one of the reasons why matchplay agreed with Hagen. He refused to let anything get to him. If he hit a bad shot, it was done, history – there was nothing he could do about it. By shrugging it off he stayed relaxed, mentally sharp and thus better equipped to make sure that the next shot was a good one.

CORRECTION: Hagen's 'smell the flowers' attitude is an example to us all. If you can learn to keep your composure after the bad shots, I guarantee you'll hit fewer of them. Byron Nelson was one golfer who learnt the importance of staying cool. Early in his career he got so angry during one tournament that he threw his putter up a tree, which as you can imagine wouldn't have done his score the power of good. He vowed from there on never to let his temper get the better of him, forcing himself to breathe more slowly and even walk slowly in potentially stressful situations. Whether you choose to smell the flowers like Hagen, or breathe slowly like Nelson, it's entirely up to you. What is important is that you find a way, any way, of staying calm on the golf course. Because the minute you lose your cool, you stop thinking clearly. And that's when you make big mistakes.

On a personal note, when I played in the 1950s and early 1960s I occasionally became very annoyed with myself. If I were playing today I would enlist the help of a sports psychologist, as do many of today's golfers.

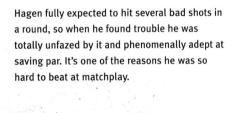

Hagen fully expected to hit several bad shots in a round, so when he found trouble he was totally unfazed by it and phenomenally adept at saving par. It's one of the reasons he was so hard to beat at matchplay.

Ben Hogan

The story of Ben Hogan is so remarkable that it is hardly surprising Hollywood made a film about his life. As a boy he endured the agony of seeing his father shoot himself. As a young professional he struggled to make his way and, just when he was riding high, he was nearly killed in a car crash. He then rebuilt himself to become the greatest ball-striker who ever picked up a golf club. There'll never be another Ben Hogan.

Let me tell you a tale that illustrates how good Ben Hogan was. When he won the 1953 Open at Carnoustie – the only time he played in our championship – the draw for the last day wasn't like it is now, leaders out last. Instead, we played 36 holes on the final day and the order of play was determined by drawing names out of the hat. As luck would have it, during both the morning and afternoon rounds I was waiting to play on the third tee when Hogan was hitting down the par-five sixth. The two tees are close together and I had a view straight down his target line. For those who don't know Carnoustie, there is out of bounds all the way down the left of the sixth hole and a bunker about a third of the way into the fairway on that side. Then there is two-thirds of fairway to the right of that bunker and some shortish rough right of that. Everybody took the safe option, either aiming at the middle of the fairway, looking to fade it away from the bunker and the out of bounds fence, or aiming into the right-hand rough and playing for a little draw.

Everybody except Hogan, that is.

I can assure readers now that he was the only man in the field, and I mean the only man, who aimed at that tiny gap between the bunker and the out-of-bounds fence. His lightning-quick swing fired the ball off on that line like a bullet, and towards the end of it's flight there was just the merest hint of fade which brought the ball round the back of the bunker and into middle of the fairway. That was the only way you could knock it on the green in two that day,

because a ditch ran across the fairway, arcing nearer to the tee the further right you went. So while we were hitting lofted woods or irons to lay up short of the ditch on the right-hand side of the fairway, Hogan took a driver on a narrow line that no one else dared contemplate, which put the green in range. He made birdie-fours both times, shot 70-68 and won by four shots.

This was Hogan at his sublime best. Aged 41, he entered only six tournaments that year and won five of them. Three of the five were major championships – the Open, US Open and US Masters. How about that?

It had been a long, hard road to the top, though. After his father committed suicide, the family struggled financially. So at the age of 11 Ben decided he could earn some extra money by caddying at the local golf course in Fort Worth, Texas where another young boy called Byron Nelson also caddied. At the age of 15 the two of them tied for first place with scores of 39 over nine holes in the club's inaugural annual caddies' tournament. Nelson won the sudden-death playoff and that proved to be something of an omen for years to come because while Nelson was enjoying success relatively quickly as a professional, Hogan was struggling just to make ends meet.

Considering what we now know about Hogan's career, it's almost impossible to believe that he went nearly 10 years without even a sniff of victory. But that was precisely how it was. Every time Hogan tried his hand on tour, he ran out of money and had to head home for the security of a club pro's job. It would have broken many lesser men, but Hogan's strength of mind always was one of

the best clubs in his bag. His persistence paid off and in 1938, again down to literally his last few dollars, he came second in a tournament and won nearly $300. That unspectacular cheque transformed Hogan's fortunes. As well as putting food on the table and petrol in the tank of his car, it bought him precious time on tour. He made the most of it and within a few years he was the leading money winner in the United States.

I remember reading once how he'd said: "My greatest accomplishment was being able to make a living playing golf after going broke twice starting out."

Making a living? Hmm, that has to be the all-time classic understatement. By the mid-1940s he was the best player in the world, no question about it. Twice he registered double-digit tournament wins in a single season. Then came the car crash, the life-threatening injuries and the remarkable recovery. It is amazing that he lived through that at all – his injuries were so dire that the local paper in Texas even distributed Hogan's obituary to the TV and Radio stations in the area. But not only did Hogan live through it, he rebuilt himself to become an even better player, winning six majors in the first four years after his return from injury. An astonishing strike rate.

He had a reputation for being cold and unfriendly, but I met enough people who spoke of Hogan's warm side to believe otherwise. During the Open at Carnoustie he and I had adjoining lockers and far from being the cold man that many portrayed him to be, I can say that he seemed quite the opposite. I'm not saying he was a real talker, because he wasn't. But every time he walked into the locker room he would smile warmly and say "Good morning, young man."

On the course it was a different story. Certainly anyone troubled by Hogan's apparent frostiness off the course would have been chilled to the bone by the ice-cold look in his eyes in the heat of competition. No one was more cool under pressure than Hogan – he would have made Jack Frost sweat. During Open week at Carnoustie the Scots nicknamed him the 'Wee Ice Mon.'

Other golfers won more tournaments than Ben Hogan, but none commanded greater respect. For many, he was and always will be the ultimate ball-striker.

13: The grip so often holds the key to curing a hook

DIAGNOSIS: One of Hogan's famous quotes was about the dreaded hook that once plagued his game. "I hate a hook. It nauseates me. I could vomit when I see one." That's a pretty scathing remark by any standards. But that was how Ben felt about his golf. Perfection was his passion and a hook was an obstacle to this dream. Byron Nelson, a fellow boyhood caddie and contemporary back in Texas, had an explanation as to the origin of Hogan's hated hook, namely, that being a relatively small boy he developed a strong grip in order to be able to hit a low hook off the tee that went a long way. Whatever the reason, it became a persistent and irritating fault well into adulthood.

EXPLANATION: I had long chats about Hogan with Byron Nelson and he revealed to me that before the car crash in 1949 Hogan had always played with a strong four-knuckle grip. I knew this from studying his game, but what I didn't know was that for many years Hogan used to practice with a weak two-knuckle grip. But, as Byron explained, as soon as Ben stepped on to the first tee in a tournament he went straight back to his strong grip which he felt he could trust. It was only during his enforced lay-off after the car crash that he came to the conclusion that if ever he could play golf again, he'd make sure he not only practiced with a weakish grip, but played like that also. It was the only way he could see to get rid of his hook.

Ben's weak grip and fanning-open of the clubface in the takeaway meant that he could swish the club as hard and fast as he liked through impact, without any fear of hitting a hook. When the ball left the clubface it was like a bullet being fired from a rifle.

CORRECTION: It was an inspired decision, because Hogan went from good to great when he changed his grip. While we consider what we can learn from him, it is important that we look not at the grip in isolation, but how he used the grip to determine the clubface positioning, which in turn dictates the flight of the ball.

Be careful all you slicers out there. The forthcoming lesson is most definitely not for you. With a weak left-hand grip, Hogan fanned the clubface in the takeaway and cupped his left wrist at the top, which meant the face was distinctly open throughout his swing. Therefore he could swish the clubhead through the ball as fast as he liked and the ball wouldn't go left. This is why he was the only golfer in the field at the Carnoustie Open who had the nerve to aim at an out of bounds fence. He knew he couldn't hook it because he had a job just getting the clubface nearly square at impact.

Interestingly enough, Hogan's weak left-hand grip also incorporated a short left thumb position. I've found that a short left thumb promotes a hook in most club golfers, but Hogan felt that it helped him stop hooking. I would maintain that Hogan is the exception as far as this rule is concerned. I've taught no end of people and stopped them hooking the ball by lengthening their left thumb. I'm sticking to that theory now, because a longer left thumb connects the hands to the wrists and forearms more effectively and cuts down on a lot of independent hand action through impact. You might like to experiment with both positions and see which one works for you. Remember to bear in mind another of Hogan's great lines, though: "If a grip change doesn't feel awful then you haven't made a grip change at all." In golf, any meaningful changes require perseverance.

I saw a lot of Hogan at Carnoustie in 1953 and my abiding impression was the speed at which he unwound his hips in the downswing. He used to say: "You cannot spin out too quickly in the downswing." He was referring to the hips and it emphasizes how there was no thought in his mind of any lateral movement in this area.

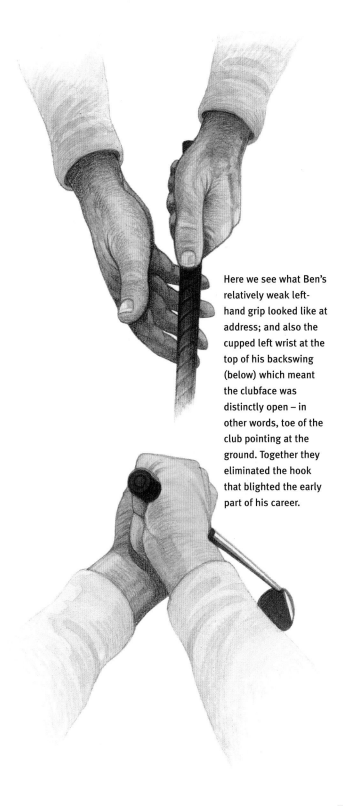

Here we see what Ben's relatively weak left-hand grip looked like at address; and also the cupped left wrist at the top of his backswing (below) which meant the clubface was distinctly open – in other words, toe of the club pointing at the ground. Together they eliminated the hook that blighted the early part of his career.

14: Rhythm – do it your own sweet way

DIAGNOSIS: You may have seen pictures of Hogan, but you could not possibly get an idea of the speed of his swing. It was like lightning and couldn't have been in greater contrast to Sam Snead's slow, almost lazy tempo. The pace of his swing and the speed the ball shot off the clubface was like a bullet. Indeed, the ball-flight was one of the extraordinary things about Hogan's game.

EXPLANATION: If you'd have tried to make Ben Hogan slow down his swing and Sam Snead speed up his, you'd have never heard of either of them. Snead would have probably been a farmer, Hogan a professional poker player – those steely-blue eyes wouldn't have given much away! The thing is, both players swung the club at a pace that felt right for them and, more importantly, at a pace

that allowed them to stay in complete control. They also had wonderful balance.

CORRECTION: Your best rhythm is one which allows you to generate power, while maintaining complete control over the many moving parts in your golf swing. As I've explained, everyone is different and therefore I believe that even the experienced golfer will benefit from a little trial and error in this department. Next time you practice, hit batches of balls with different-paced swings. Start with your normal rhythm and experiment on both the fast and slow side of that. By working on different rhythms you'll soon get a feeling for the ideal blend of power, control and balance. That's the rhythm for you.

A great deal also depends on the type of person you

are. If you're hyper-active, a fast walker and talker, then the chances are your optimum swing speed will be on the Hogan side of rapid. If you're more of a laid-back type, someone who walks slowly and seldom gets flustered, then I would say your golf swing's ideal operating speed will be on the slow side, rather like a Fred Couples or a Vijay Singh. Lastly, fast swingers are invariably short in stature – slow swingers are usually much taller. I think this may be due in part to differences in the centre of gravity.

These are mere indicators, though, the rules are by no means set in stone. As I will remind you many times in this book, trial and error is one of golf's greatest teachers.

The rhythm of Ben's swing was very fast indeed. But the moving parts were completely in control and he was blessed with nothing less than perfect balance. It matters not whether you swing as fast as Ben, or much slower, merely that your rhythm allows you to generate power while staying in complete control of your swing. That is the essence of good rhythm.

Hale Irwin

In his prime Hale Irwin had the bespectacled, studious look of a bank clerk. But that was only ever accurate in as much as he became used to handling heaps of dollar bills, which came his way by virtue of a superb and enduring golf game.

Of all the fine golfers of the modern era Hale Irwin must be close-to-unique in having never needed a teacher or coach to keep his good looking, sound golf swing in perfect working order. Let's disregard his technique for a minute, though, because if we are looking for clues to the secret of Hale's success we need look no further than the six inches between his ears. Temperament is the best club in Hale's bag. Self control, concentration and 100 per cent thoughtful application – these are the virtues which turned a steady player into something special.

I can't help but think back to the 1983 Open at Royal Birkdale, where he finished runner-up by a single shot to Tom Watson. Midway through the third round he fresh-aired a two-inch putt, but did he blow a fuse? Of course not. Whereas some fine players would have disappeared off the leaderboard in a fit of pique, Hale stayed calm, even though inside I'm sure he was furious with himself for being so careless, and just got on with it without a word of complaint. This is one of the great qualities that Hale shares with the likes of Jack Nicklaus, Tom Watson and more recently Ernie Els. They never get down on their luck or complain about bad breaks or silly mistakes. To these fine champions, the next shot is the only shot that matters.

Hale's strength of character also came to the fore on tough championship courses, where any cracks in a golfer's armour tend to be ruthlessly punished. Indeed the tougher the courses got the more Hale seemed to like it, which is why he managed to win three US Opens, a tally bettered by only four men in history. The first was in 1974 and the last in 1990 when at the age of 45 he holed a mammoth putt across the 18th green, galloped around on a lap of honour reminiscent of a man half his age, then came back down to earth to win the playoff the following day.

Hale always was very strong in head-to-head combat. In the mid-1970s he won back-to-back World Matchplay championships, ending Gary Player's domination of the event, and only a sudden-death playoff could deny him a hat-trick of titles. In five Ryder Cup teams he was unbeaten in 15 of his 20 matches. Mind you, victory in one of those 15 matches was handed to him on a plate. It was the 1979 Ryder Cup at The Greenbrier when he and Tom Kite played against Des Smyth and Ken Brown. Ken hit a bad second shot into the first green and being the volatile young man that he was back then, wouldn't speak to his partner or anyone else for the rest of the round, which actually didn't end up being very long because they lost 7&6. I went up to Hale afterwards and apologized for Ken's behaviour and for them not putting up a stronger show and he just smiled and replied: "Oh, don't worry John. It was perfect for us."

If temperament is Hale's best club, the mid-irons and long-irons are a close second. He was awesome in that department, which in a sense was just as well because he wasn't a long hitter. On the rare occasions he did miss a green he was such a marvellous chipper that he always seemed to get it up and down in two. Hale's sharpness doesn't seem to have faded with the passing of the years, either. He was a good enough player to win the US Tour's Heritage Classic in his 49th year and to be honest I think he could have won even more events on the main tour if he had put his mind to it.

Instead when he turned 50 he took up his playing rights on the US Senior Tour and, let's not beat around the bush here, simply annihilated the opposition. In 1998 alone he won almost $3 million, winning seven tournaments and finishing in the top five in all but two of the 22 events he played in. That brought his tally in two seasons to 16 tournament wins, suggesting that not only were his skills intact, but also the mental intensity that made him such a good player in the first place. "Some people may be happy going out and playing golf and getting their money," he said in 1998. "But that's not how I live my life. I love the competition. I feel alive when I'm competing."

At the time of writing, Hale is the biggest money winner in history, having sailed past the $13 million mark. We always pass the time of day whenever we see each other. Next time we meet I think I'll ask to borrow a fiver!

15: Feet together gets hands and arms swinging freely

DIAGNOSIS: Hale has always turned his shoulders very correctly, but occasionally the club tends to follow the body a little too closely for comfort, which means the hands and arms finish the backswing a fraction flat. From there his hands, arms and shoulders are inclined to start down a little bit locked together which means Hale is slightly over the top as he starts his downswing and thus the club is slightly outside the line.

EXPLANATION: Hale knows his golf swing better than anyone and thus would have been forever mindful of this tendency. An incident in the mid-1980s would confirm this to be the case. I'd flown out to one of my golf schools in the States and on my arrival discovered that Hale had been

Here we see from Hale the correct blend of a relatively flat shoulder turn, with the left arm on a slightly more upright plane.

practicing at the club for two whole weeks, hitting balls for six hours a day every day, and not once did he hit a shot other than with his feet together. Now bear in mind this is a multiple US Open champion and one of the best players in the world, yet he didn't once hit a regular full shot. That's patience and dedication for you. His practice routine struck a chord with me because when I was combining the roles of tour professional and teaching professional at Sandy Lodge in Hertfordshire I used to hit balls with my feet together for at least an hour a day. I'll explain to you now why it can be such a useful exercise.

CORRECTION: One of the most common mistakes among club golfers in my lifetime is they finish the backswing with their shoulders, which makes the swing too flat, and start the downswing with their shoulders, which throws the club away from the body and outside the ideal downswing plane. In simple terms, they apply the body too much, too early in the downswing. Hale occasionally suffers from a mild case of this problem.

Hale would spend hour after hour hitting shots from a narrow stance to encourage his hands and arms to swing more freely. This is a great exercise for anyone who slices the ball, since it cures the problem of starting the downswing with the shoulders.

For anyone who shares this tendency, hitting shots from a very narrow stance is perfect medicine because it encourages you to swing the club down as opposed to swinging yourself. It gets the hands and arms working and promotes a much more free swish of the club down and through. If you start to drift back into old habits and apply too much body action from the top, you very quickly lose your balance.

Next time you're at the range, hit a mid-iron shot with your feet close together. If you lose your balance in the downswing, that's a sign you're applying too much body action. So, get your feet together and point the club at the target at the top of the backswing. As you change direction feel that your hands and arms start down first and that the body stays 'quiet'. Think of the action of a fisherman casting a fly, because there are certain similarities. You don't apply your body to send the fly out towards the water. Instead, you draw your arm back and, as the fly is still moving backwards you move your arm towards the water and then the hand and wrist apply the

power – there's a moment's lag as you change direction, like a delayed reaction. That's the feeling you want as you start your downswing in golf. There's real softness in the hands and wrists at this point. Nothing stiff or wooden.

Finally a word about the mental side of the game. Think back to the tiny putt Hale missed in the 1983 Open and learn from the way he dealt with that. Some golfers would have reacted badly and disappeared without trace. But he kept his composure, went on to shoot a level par 72 that day and followed it up with a 67 in the final round to put himself right in the frame. Tom Watson denied him with a brilliant and composed finish, but the point is, Hale was in there with a chance of winning. When things go wrong for you in a competition – say, you get a bad bounce or you make a stupid mistake – don't let it ruin your entire round. Learn to put it behind you and get on with the game. The next shot is the only shot that matters. It's easier said than done, of course, but I believe if you work at it you can develop a better temperament on the golf course and that can only be of benefit to your scores.

Tony Jacklin

When the 20th century draws to a close, Tony Jacklin will find himself alone in the privileged company of Harry Vardon as a Brit who simultaneously held the Open Championship and US Open titles. And like Vardon, he was a tremendous competitor.

For 12 inspired months Tony Jacklin had the confidence and the look of the best player in the world. I'll never forget walking the final round at Royal Lytham when he won the Open in 1969. Most people remember that win for dear old Henry Longhurst's famous description of Tony's drive at the 18th: "What a corker." Well, his entire round was quite the most courageous you could ever wish to see, because at that time Tony wasn't quite as good a player as he thought he was. But he was strong and absolutely fearless. He looked every shot and every putt straight in the eye and didn't shy away from the challenge. That's what I call a champion's temperament.

By the time he went to play in the US Open the following summer, Tony was a different player. His swing had become distinctly more correct and that meant he had a golf game that more than lived up to his expectations. This formidable collection of assets elevated his game to a sublime level and he won the title by an almost unthinkable seven shots. It was the biggest winning margin in more than half-a-century of US Opens and it meant that Tony was the first British player since Harry Vardon in 1900 to hold the US Open and Open Championship titles. The lorry driver's son from Scunthorpe had become every bit the high roller.

When in 1970 he rolled into St Andrews to defend his Open title, he was greeted like a returning hero. No doubt swept along to some extent by the wave of home support, Tony raced to the turn in 29 shots and then birdied the 10th to go eight under par. Soon after that putt dropped, though, Lady Luck left town and in off the North Sea rode a dark, violent storm. Play was suspended for the day and it had the equivalent effect of an 800-metre runner being tripped coming down the back straight – all momentum was lost. When Tony resumed play the next day, alas the magic had been washed away with the rain and he slumped to probably the most depressing 67 a man could ever shoot.

He finished fifth that year and in years to come had several other near misses that could have been victories, had it not been for the intervention of Lee Trevino. Some say that Trevino's multiple chip-in escapades ruined Tony's career. But I'm not so sure. By then, Tony had started chasing the big money that his management group set up for him as Open champion, and being a working-class lad he quite understandably wasn't going

to turn that down. Personally I think this punishing, globe-trotting schedule took its toll on his golf. Perhaps more significantly, Tony's sweet putting stroke turned sour. That was one of the reasons he'd been such a great champion in the first place – although his stylish swing partly overshadowed that part of his game – but once the putts stopped dropping, so did his earnings. Although he won the PGA Championship in 1982, aged 37, he wasn't the same player. If his putting had held up, there's no question in my mind that Tony's playing career would have been far more enduring.

As it was, his career took a different turn. Whereas in the sixties and seventies he let his clubs do the talking, in the 1980s he used a 'walky-talky' to call the shots, masterminding Europe's Ryder Cup renaissance, which began with victory at the Belfry in 1985. You have to say it was a good time to be in charge, with the likes of Seve Ballesteros, Nick Faldo, Bernhard Langer, Sandy Lyle and Ian Woosnam at the height of their powers, but Tony was a strong and influential captain who found a way of bringing out the collective best in a group of brilliant individuals.

Aside from that, I always admired him because he had the guts and courage to step out of a poor boy's background and take on the world. He'd been a brilliant amateur, winning the Lincolnshire Boys title at just 13, and was Rookie of the Year when he turned pro aged 18.

I remember in the late 1960s when Tony first tried his hand on the US Tour. He was determined to prove himself at the highest level, for in his mind the sooner he learned to play against the best, the sooner he'd learn to beat them. He was right. When he won the Jacksonville Open in 1968, it gave him the confidence to believe that he was as good as anyone. For a brief spell afterwards, Tony was more than that. He was better than anyone.

16: Here's hope for all you left-to-right slicers

DIAGNOSIS: The first lesson I ever gave Tony Jacklin was in 1967 at Royal Lytham during the old Pringle tournament. I was doing some commentary on behalf of ITV for their Saturday afternoon *World of Sport* program. At the time I didn't know Tony that well, other than to say hello, but he came up to me on the Friday night and asked me if I'd look at his swing the next morning. I said I'd be delighted to and remember telling him then that I thought he 'had it all' but his swing just wasn't quite good enough.

Back then the final two rounds of a tournament were played on Saturdays. Tony was some way behind the leaders and had an early tee time, so I got up at the crack of dawn to meet him on the practice ground before he went out. Straight away his problems were obvious. He was standing open-shouldered at address, taking the club back on the inside which made his backswing very flat, then looping it over the top on the way down. Consequently he was hitting a lot of his drives with a left-to-right cut and also some of his shots out of the heel.

EXPLANATION: This was classic 'cause and effect'. Tony's set-up was very open which ordinarily promotes an outside-the-line takeaway. To counter this, the brain subconsciously sends urgent messages to get the club back on the inside as soon as possible in the takeaway,

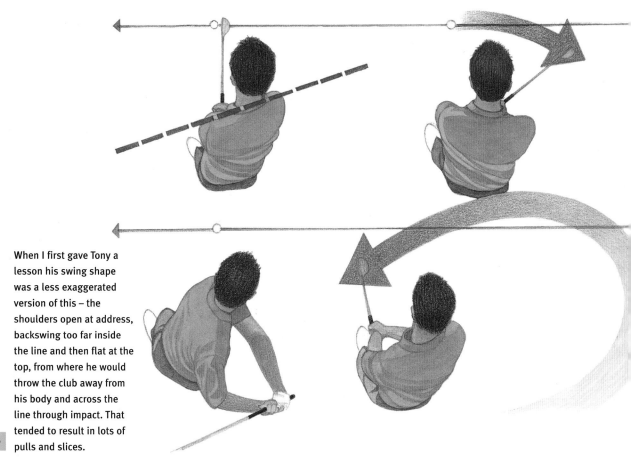

When I first gave Tony a lesson his swing shape was a less exaggerated version of this – the shoulders open at address, backswing too far inside the line and then flat at the top, from where he would throw the club away from his body and across the line through impact. That tended to result in lots of pulls and slices.

but the trouble is that leads to a very flat and trapped position at the top of the backswing. The only way to go from there is to loop the club outside the line and swing across the line through impact. That's what Tony was doing and thus most of his shots were starting left and either staying left or slicing.

Fortunately, given the right medicine it's a problem easily cured. I got him to set up to the ball with his body much more square to the target line and then swing the club up on the inside, as opposed to on the inside and too flat. This gave him room at the top of his backswing to swing the club down on the correct path into and through impact.

Straight after that practice session he went out and shot two great scores in very trying conditions, putting him in the clubhouse miles ahead of anyone else who was out on the course. I promise you the tournament was virtually over bar the shouting, before *World of Sport* had even gone on the air! The producers were none too happy.

CORRECTION: That fault in Tony's swing has for many years been a common problem at club level. It's what you might call a 'figure-of-eight' slicer's swing and anyone suffering from it will hit lots of drives that start left and slice. If that sounds worryingly familiar, the lesson I gave Tony Jacklin all those years ago is the one I'd give you if you were stood in front of me now.

Set up with your shoulders aligned square, or if anything feel that they aim a little to the right, then swing the club back upwards, as well as on the inside. In order to make a difference you'll have to feel that your hands are reaching for the sky, although you mustn't forget to turn your shoulders. This puts you in a position at the top of your backswing where there is much more daylight between your arms and your body. So suddenly you have much more room to swing the club down on the correct path. And remember, angle of attack is directly influenced by swing path. So by improving your swing path you also improve your angle of attack. You'll sweep the ball away which results in more solid, on-line drives.

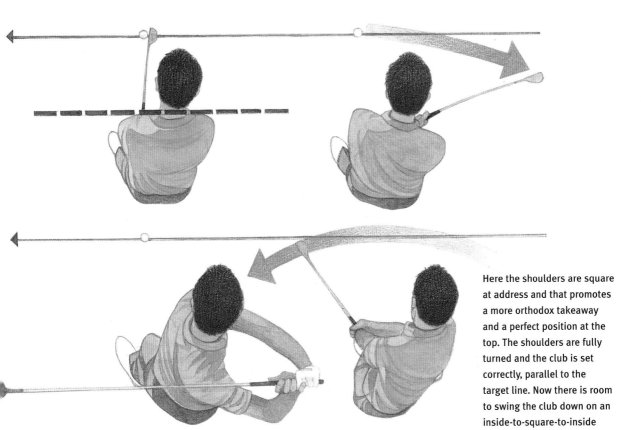

Here the shoulders are square at address and that promotes a more orthodox takeaway and a perfect position at the top. The shoulders are fully turned and the club is set correctly, parallel to the target line. Now there is room to swing the club down on an inside-to-square-to-inside path, producing more solid, straight shots.

Bobby Jones

Winner of three Opens, four US Opens, one British Amateur and five US Amateurs – all before he reached the age of 30. And he wasn't even playing for money. No wonder some say that Bobby Jones was the greatest golfer of all time.

Some of my earliest memories are of my father talking about the remarkable exploits of Bobby Jones. Even after I had started playing the game, when Henry Cotton had become very much the man of the moment, people would still speak in awe and admiration of the great Bobby Jones. Indeed, many a year would have to pass before people stopped saying to any talented youngster who started to show promise: "Now then young man, are you going to be another Bob Jones?"

Of course, the more I learnt about golf the more I started to appreciate how much this remarkable man had achieved in his short but spectacular career and why he left such an indelible mark on the consciousness of all who saw him play. I've watched his classic video tapes dozens of times and marvelled at his gorgeous, rounded, fluent, long golf swing. It was quite a rapid swing by any standards, but the wonderful rhythm and exquisite timing made a metronome look out of kilter. Add this to a sublime and sensitive touch on the greens, using his famous Calamity Jane putter, and one can start to understand just how great Bobby Jones was.

He was I think quite unique among the truly great golfers who dominated the game during the first third of the century in as much that he didn't come from a poor background. Far from it, in fact. Jones was born into a wealthy family in Atlanta. However, any potential childhood fiscal gains were more than cancelled out by

physical pains.

Young Robert Tyre Jones was a sickly boy and there were times when his illnesses were bad enough to be life-threatening.

But although lacking in physical strength, right from an early age Jones was clearly a natural athlete with a wonderful eye for a ball. He took to golf straight away and was scoring in the 70s before he'd even reached his teenage years. By the time he was 15 he had become the youngest ever US Southern Amateur champion – a diminutive figure of a boy competing and succeeding in a distinctly grown-up world. Greatness seemed to lie just around the corner, but for some strange reason Jones missed the turning and rather lost his way. Everyone expected him to dominate the amateur game, but in five years he failed to win a single big tournament.

Those backward steps in his late teens were swiftly wiped out with giant leaps forward in his early twenties. The frailty of youth was gone and Jones had developed into a strong young man. His first big tournament win was the 1923 US Open – not such a bad way to open your account. From then on he seemed like a young man in an awful hurry, winning not just ordinary tournaments, but Majors, with astonishing regularity.

In 1930 Jones exceeded even his own remarkable standards winning (and I suggest you sit down for this) the British Amateur Championship, the Open Championship, the US Open and the US Amateur Championship – the Impregnable Quadrilateral as it was dubbed by one New York journalist. He was 28 years old and, in surely the greatest ever example of quitting while one is ahead, retired from competitive golf.

It must have come as a surprise to many people, but Jones had no money worries and thus the tug of the professional game was non-existent. Besides, he always maintained that his family came first, then his career as a lawyer and then his golf, which he considered only a game and certainly not a means of making a living.

What he deprived the golfing world of in playing terms, though, he repaid in the form of his wondrous creation. It started when he and a business partner bought a plot of land in Augusta, Georgia. At the time it was a fruit farm, but Jones had grander visions. He enlisted the services of the great architect Alister Mackenzie and together they created Augusta National Golf Club. The original idea was that it should be a place where Jones, an essentially shy character, could play golf with his friends in private, away from the adoring fans who flocked in their thousands to see him whenever he teed-up. But as we now know, of course, Jones' idea of an exclusive invitational tournament soon became golf's fourth major – the US Masters.

By the time I had turned professional, Jones was already not a well man, suffering from a cruel and debilitating illness that eventually confined him to a wheelchair. It is always tragic whenever a human being suffers such misfortune, but somehow the effects seem more acute when a great athlete is the victim. Although deprived of the pleasure of playing golf, Jones could at least enjoy an active interest at The Masters, the tournament he helped to initiate on the golf course he helped to build, almost up to the time when he died at the age of 69.

When I look back at the achievements of Bobby Jones, I see a record that will surely never be bettered. Quite apart from the four US Open wins, he was runner-up in another three. And in six Walker Cups, he played 11 matches, won 10, lost one. We can only hazard a guess as to what Jones might have achieved had he continued playing golf into his thirties. Perhaps he, rather than Jack Nicklaus, would be the one now sitting on top in the list of major winners.

17: Comfortable isn't necessarily correct

DIAGNOSIS: Bobby Jones had such a lovely fluent, confident, letting-go golf swing. By 'letting-go' I mean the clubhead really free-wheeled through the ball. Indeed, I remember reading in one of Jones' books that he felt the clubhead reached maximum speed prior to impact, then free-wheeled into the back of the ball. I must say, I like the sound of that – it seems to me to conjure up the sort of freedom of movement in the downswing that many club golfers could aspire to. More of a swing rather than a hit, if you like.

Much of this technique could be attributed to the young Bobby Jones watching, and probably to a degree modelling himself on, Stuart Maiden, a Scottish-born professional who had emigrated to Atlanta and become the head pro at Jones' home club at East Lake. He later became Jones' teacher and used to travel the world with him, witnessing every 'corner' of the famous Impregnable Quadrilateral year. Maiden taught Jones as simply as possible, saying that: "I knew it was a mistake to confuse him with too many things." Actually Jones knew a great deal about the swing and later wrote brilliantly about every facet of the game, but Maiden's teaching style obviously worked for him.

If Jones had a fault, it was that the ball forever kept creeping back in his stance. Always conscious of this, Maiden used to say to him in his own

There was a wonderful sense of fluidity about Bobby Jones' swing, he really free-wheeled the club into the back of the ball generating fantastic speed. It was a definite swing rather than a hit, which is a good point for the club golfer to bear in mind.

If the ball is too far back in the stance the clubhead is travelling in-to-out at impact, which means every shot starts right. Too far forward and the clubhead is travelling out-to-in at impact which means the ball starts left.

charming way, "Now Mr Jones, ball forward in your stance a bit, please. Come on, just a bit more than that." He had to gently coax him into the correct position, because Jones used to feel comfortable with the ball too far back in his stance. Most of us are the same – the ball feels best when it's in the middle of our stance because we feel we can hit it from there, but we can't hit it straight from there. We tend to push it or hook it. It's one example of why 'comfortable' isn't always 'correct'.

EXPLANATION: The golfers who should really keep an eye out for this fault are those who tend to hook the ball, because this type of shot-pattern is invariably caused by the ball being too far back in the stance. As I've said, it feels comfortable, but the problem is caused because the clubhead meets the ball before it has reached the on-line part of its swing. It's travelling in-to-out, so you invariably hit it straight right or with a big hook.

   Slicers will have the opposite problem. Their tendency will be to let the ball creep too far forward in the stance, which means the clubhead has travelled beyond the on-line portion of its swing path and is thus swinging left of target at impact. That's where the pull or the big slice originates from.

CORRECTION: So how can you take something from the great Bobby Jones and use it to the benefit of your own game? Well, the first thing to do is identify your shot pattern. Are you typically a slicer or a hooker of the ball? Then get someone to study your ball position with the driver. If it is incorrectly positioned, you need to be coaxed into the correct position. Coaxing is what Maiden had to do with Jones and it's the teaching method I have to adopt because ball back in the stance does tend to feel ever-so comfortable, especially among good players. Jose Maria Olazabal is the same. He sometimes needs a little more than mere coaxing, so I often say quite firmly: "C'mon, we're not in the Ryder Cup now – just hit the

thing." So he does and bang, he hits the perfect drive, followed by another and then another. Only then is he ever convinced.

   Do please bear in mind, however, that changing ball position is one of those things that takes some doing. Don't immediately expect it to feel right and comfortable because it won't. As I often say to pupils, improving your golf swing involves putting up with a bit of discomfort, because if you change anything meaningful that is how the first shots will feel. As long as you remember that it is far more important to be correct than it is to be comfortable, you will always stand a chance of fulfilling your potential.

Tom Kite

When the Kite family moved to a new house in Austin, Texas, in the early 1960s, young Tom begged his father to build a putting green in the back garden and made sure it was floodlit, too. Not even darkness was going to get in the way of his selfless work ethic and overwhelming desire to succeed, qualities that would later bring much glory and gold.

It's uncanny how throughout history some great golfing rivalries have been established at a young age and then sustained all the way to the highest level. Such was the fate of Tom Kite, who as a boy growing up in Austin, Texas, competed against Ben Crenshaw. I remember reading a great story about how in their first ever game together, the 13-year-old Tom moved so much earth with his first swing that the clubhead literally bounced over the ball. "I could have crawled into the divot," Tom admitted years later.

There can't have been too many shots like that, though, because Tom and Ben were the star college

golfers of their generation, between them winning 12 of the 13 events played in one year and sharing the national college championship in 1972. The following year, Tom was Rookie of the Year on the US Tour and a year later Ben followed suit. When Ben holed his epic putt on 10th green on the way to victory in the 1984 Masters, who was watching from the middle of the fairway? Tom, who else!

They have shared so much, including the same mentor Harvey Penick, yet the two of them could scarcely be more different. Ben is the archetypal, good-looking, natural athlete, an artist who looks like he plays golf with about as much scientific analysis as a fish swimming in water. Whereas Tom is a studious, hard-working, more

mechanical player, a grinder who to the casual observer would appear to swing by numbers. That would be an unfair assumption, because Tom is an exceptionally talented golfer. But it's an accurate analysis in the sense that Tom has always been the kind of person who needed to understand everything about his swing. To him knowledge is reassurance, which is why he has throughout his career felt at home on the practice range.

Years of thoughtful application are reflected in Tom's golf swing. He fulfils the four impact factors, that I mentioned in my introduction, perfectly. He delivers the clubhead into the back of the ball absolutely bang square and on the perfect path, which in his prime meant he was deceptively long off the tee. There isn't one bit of wasted energy in his swing. Indeed, his swing is so correct and so lacking in flamboyancy that you could say he plays a type of game that is actually quite boring to watch. I don't mean that in a derogatory way, though, and I'd be very hard-pushed to criticize even one aspect of his golf swing.

Also, he knew his limitations in the sense that he was a brilliant course manager. You'd never see him trying the impossible shots. This is why Tom was for so many years a serial top-10 finisher, doing so many things well and not making stupid tactical errors meant that he hardly ever shot a big score. Tom is also one of the most competitive people you could ever come up against, which is part of the reason he is one of the most successful Ryder Cup players ever, unbeaten in seven singles matches (won five, halved two). I remember when poor Howard Clark was on the wrong side of Tom's brilliance at The Belfry in 1989 losing 8&7 which I think is the heaviest defeat in the singles. Tom was massively under-par, without looking like he was doing anything very special. That's one of the

reasons why Tom is underrated. He goes about his business quietly, but with great purpose. I think that's very impressive.

By the mid-1990s Kite was the leading money winner of all time, but he didn't have a major to his name and, worse than that, he'd let a few slip that deep down he probably knew he should have won. In hindsight, Tom admits: "That bugged the daylights out of me... the longer it went, the more I wanted to win." But at the age of 42 he finally applied his considerable experience to positive effect, winning the 1992 US Open at Pebble Beach. After all those years of hard work, he grinded out a victory in the toughest of conditions. It was just how you'd imagine Tom winning a major.

Perhaps we should have guessed that a man named Kite would choose one of the windiest last days of a major championship on which to achieve his lifetime goal. It is a mark of the man that Tom couldn't wait to get the trophy back to Harvey Penick's house and into his old mentor's hands. A nice touch, I thought.

18: Balance flat shoulder turn with upright arm swing

DIAGNOSIS: The first time I saw Tom play was during the Walker Cup match at St Andrews in 1971. Unsurprisingly for one growing up in the Nicklaus era of domination, he was what I call a 'rocker and blocker', swinging the club too straight with the body tilting, as were three or four youngsters in that team. As soon as I saw them on the practice ground I said to the captain of the GB&I team Michael Bonallack: "You've got a hell of a chance of winning this match." That's because a 'rock and block' swing is only effective if the fairways are lush and the ball sits up. But this was The Old Course in May, before any new season growth, bare and bone-hard under foot. There was no way many of that US team could avoid hitting the occasional shot a bit thin and sure enough, when the match got underway, I sat behind the 18th green and almost lost count of the number of times they thinned approach shots to the back of the green and three-putted. They could not get the clubhead to the bottom of the ball with their pitch shots. That's the problem with a rock and block swing – the angle of attack

won't let you get ball-turf contact. It would be alright if the game was all about driving off a tee-peg. But it isn't.

The Americans did indeed lose that Walker Cup match, their first defeat in more than 30 years. I sat down with a few of their team afterwards and explained to them the fact that the swing is not a straight line and that the sooner they stopped rocking and blocking the better they would play. To Tom's great credit, when I next saw him a few years later his swing was completely orthodox. I take no credit for this improvement, I mention it merely to highlight what a tremendous amount of work Tom must have put in to make that kind of difference. It sums up his dedicated attitude to golf.

EXPLANATION: I can usually tell how someone swings the club just by the area of ground they choose to hit from on the practice ground. If someone is out there looking for the most lush bit of grass, they're a rocker and blocker, just as the young team members of the US 1971 Walker Cup team were. If someone throws the balls down

Few golfers have worked harder on their game than Tom Kite. The result is a swing devoid of wasted energy, so totally orthodox and under control that I suppose you could say it lacks flair.

on any bit of bare ground, this usually means they hit it from out-to-in with a steep angle of attack and they will thus struggle with the longer clubs and be better with the short irons.

CORRECTION: Which type of practicer are you? The answer to that question will tell you a lot about your swing and specifically your clubhead angle of attack. If you don't mind hitting off a tight lie, your swing is probably too steep and you need to shallow it out by hitting shots with the ball above the level of your feet, to encourage the feeling of your body turning and the arms swinging more around you instead of straight up and under.

If you like hitting off a lush lie and your game is characterized by decent driving but poor pitching, you are probably 'rocking and blocking' which is causing the clubhead's arc to bottom out before it gets to the golf ball. Hence you are fine when the ball is teed-up, because you can catch it on the upswing. But whenever the ball is on anything less than a perfect lie in the fairway, you can only hit it fat or thin. You need to get the body turning and the arms swinging up in such a way that the clubhead

travels on an inside-to-square-to-inside path through impact. That's inside as it approaches impact, square at impact, then inside again through impact.

It's important you understand that the golf swing is upright since the ball is on the ground. Many players confuse upright with straight, which the swing is certainly not. Although the swing is upright, the fact that the ball is to the side of you requires the body turn to create the necessary in-to-straight-to-in arc through the ball, the only arc which consistently can apply the clubhead correctly to the ball. When I say correctly, I mean the clubface is under control, the swing path is on-line at the moment of impact, the angle of attack is such that the bottom of the swing arc coincides with the ball and, lastly, the clubhead speed is appropriate to the distance of the shot.

The straight line rock and block action – so popular when Tom was in his youth – failed to supply a consistent angle of attack. If any reader is in any doubt that the club is only on line for a very short time need only look at the divots of a good player which point to the left at the end, confirming that the club is already swinging back to the inside through the ball.

Playing shots with the ball above the level of your feet encourages you to swing the club more around yourself, which promotes a shallow, inside attack.

Bernhard Langer

As a boy from a poor family in Germany, Bernhard Langer was given four old clubs to play with. Three of them, a two-wood, three-iron and seven-iron, he learnt to wield with devastating effect. The fourth, a putter with a bent shaft, proved a little harder to master. Thus the career pattern was set for this remarkably resilient and talented golfer.

I really take my hat off to Bernhard Langer. I can't think of a comparable situation where a sportsman has come back so many times from such fundamentally damaging technical difficulties. I'm talking about the yips, just about the worst thing that can happen to a professional golfer. To suffer them once in a career would be once too often. But poor Bernhard's putting stroke has been afflicted at least three times, the effects sometimes lasting several years. Bernhard himself describes it as "an uncontrollable movement of the muscles. It can go anywhere from a twitch, to a freeze where you can't move at all, to a sudden explosion." It's hard to imagine what that must feel like, yet easy to understand the phenomenal strength of character he has shown to overcome those physical and mental obstacles.

Much of this strength of mind can perhaps be traced back to Bernhard's childhood. Having grown up in a poor family, coping with adversity must almost have become part of the daily ritual. But from such roots do some of life's great battlers emerge and, ironically, poverty led Bernhard into the game that would one day make him a rich and remarkable man.

When he was only eight years old he asked his brother Erwin, who later became his manager, to take him to the local golf course so he could earn some pocket money as a caddie. Bernhard liked what he saw and when he was given four old clubs as a present, set about developing the technique that would take him to the top. There were no formal lessons to accelerate the learning process, instead he watched the best players at the club and picked up on the strengths in their game. Bernhard must have had discerning eyes, because he was good enough to turn professional at the age of 15, in spite of a putting stroke that was no match for his formidable long game. I remember when I was teaching the German national team in the early seventies, I had an interpreter working with me, a golf professional called Heinz Fehring. One day Heinz told me about this young assistant pro who worked for him who was "the most marvellous ball-striker, but an absolutely terrible putter." You can guess who he was talking about. It was Bernhard. He would have been only 15 or 16 years old at the time, but even then he was having trouble holing putts.

On that basis, I suppose you might say it's surprising he went on to win twice at Augusta, a golf course with

arguably the most treacherous greens in the world. But Bernhard's much-publicized traumas on the greens disguise the fact that he has at times in his career been a wonderful putter. More to the point as far as Augusta is concerned, he has also been consistently one of the best mid-iron players I've ever seen, amazingly accurate with both line and length, which means he can hit his approach shots in the right place on those vast, sloping greens thus leaving himself the most holeable putts.

This devastating accuracy is the product of a golf swing that I would describe as very sound, rather than pretty. Better to be that way round than the other, though. Dare I say Tom Weiskopf – a tall, handsome man with a lovely rhythm – was the owner of an elegant swing that wasn't quite as good as it looked. Bernhard's may look a little less classic, but if you took a picture of him at the top of his backswing, you'd see a nigh-on perfect position

which goes a long way to explain his correctness in the all-important hitting area.

At the end of the day, though, Bernhard's mental strength, which undoubtedly is much attributable to his deeply held religious conviction, is his greatest strength. Few other golfers in history could have won a tour event just days after missing that putt in the 1991 Ryder Cup at Kiawah Island and I've always admired him for his ability to compete and stay calm under pressure. And indeed for his professionalism. He leaves nothing to chance and no one prepares more thoroughly for competition. Watch him play a practice round and you can tell he's really working hard, plotting his every move like a world-class chess player. On top of all that, Bernhard is a wonderful guy, with a charm and sense of humour that alas for the general public is usually disguised by his serious 'game face'. Definitely one of Europe's finest.

19: Don't let your dominant hand take charge

DIAGNOSIS: Obviously the brain plays a part in causing the yips, but the physical culprit is independent hand and wrist action. That's what throws the putter off line with such disastrous consequences. What Bernhard has managed to do over the years is invent a series of putting strokes that all-but eliminate this problem. The most enduring was his 'clamp' grip. He would meticulously place the putter behind the ball and one-by-one the hands, arms and body slotted into position. Once his set-up was established he effectively locked everything in place, but without tension, and rocked his shoulders to make the putter flow back and forth on the ideal path. Since the hands played merely a supporting role there was very little danger of the putter-face twisting, which left only the speed of the putt to worry about. He isn't a feel putter. He's what I'd call a method putter.

EXPLANATION: The root of Bernhard's putting problems are not uncommon. If you think about it, most people who play golf right-handed are naturally right-handed and therefore there's always a real danger of your

dominant hand taking over in mid-stroke, especially in a pressurized situation. You can't afford to let that happen. Any right-hand interference upsets the rhythmical flow of the putter and destroys your ability to judge pace and line. Bernhard's answer to that challenge has at times been quite unorthodox, but it works in the sense that it takes the right hand out of the stroke and gets the shoulders, arms, hands and the putter all working together in one harmonized unit.

CORRECTION: If you are an inconsistent judger of line and length I think there is merit in some of Bernhard's methods. It doesn't really matter how you choose to form your grip, what matters is that once you have your set-up in place try to feel that you rock your shoulders in order to make the putter swing back and forth. You should sense that the triangle formed by your shoulders, arms and the club is maintained throughout, as if everything is working as a single unit, as opposed to several separate moving parts. Vary the degree of shoulder motion to control the length of your stroke and keep tension out of the equation to promote a syrupy-smooth motion.

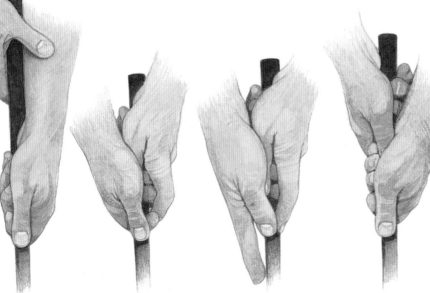

In his efforts to eliminate unwanted independent hand action, Bernhard has explored all manner of putting grips. You shouldn't be afraid to experiment, either, if it edges you closer to putting's ultimate goal, namely making your hands operate as a single unit during the stroke.

20: Separate arm-swing from shoulder-turn

DIAGNOSIS: I first met Bernhard at the Bob Hope Classic at the RAC Club in Surrey during the early 1980s. He asked me what I thought of his swing and I can remember my exact reply: "Bernhard, don't let anyone stop you turning like that." This was a time when due to a combination of the success of Jack Nicklaus and the way the swing was being taught, many players tended to rock the shoulders as opposed to turning them with just a degree of tilt established by the spine angle at address. So it made a pleasant change to see someone turning their shoulders absolutely correctly.

What I also said to Bernhard, however, was to "get your girlfriend to stand just to the right of you and behind you." I was only joking about the girlfriend, but the serious message I wanted to get across to Bernhard was that his arms were locked to his shoulder turn and he was thus swinging too flat and around himself. He needed an obstruction behind him to force him to swing his arms and the club more upwards and not so much around himself.

EXPLANATION: This isn't an unusual scenario. Often golfers suffer from the arms being locked on the same plane as the body turn, resulting in a very flat backswing. It's a position that leaves you trapped at the top, with no room to swing the club down on the correct path, resulting in anything from a bad slice to a pull hook.

CORRECTION: I don't suggest for a minute you get anyone, let alone your girlfriend or wife, to stand behind you as you swing. But if you suffer from an excessively flat swing it is a good idea when you practice to have some kind of physical presence to force you to swing the club up and on the inside in your backswing. Many a time when I was swinging too flat I would make practice swings with a hedge behind me. If I could swing the club up and avoid contact with the hedge, I knew I was getting a better balance between arm-swing and body-turn. Give it a try, but make sure you keep turning. As I said to Bernhard, you don't ever want to lose that element of your swing.

Swinging with an obstruction (such as a hedge) behind you forces the hands, arms and the club on to a more upright swing plane.

Bobby Locke

In his dominant years Bobby Locke was a distinctly unathletic figure with a unique swing and a distinct draw on his shots that probably gave the purists little pleasure. But four Open victories in under a decade speaks volumes for this mild-mannered South African's unique talent and he is undoubtedly one of the most underrated golfers of the century.

I knew Bobby Locke for many years. We first met just before the war when a grand tour of challenge matches around the country brought him to my home club, Lindrick. He was a lanky, 20-year-old kid who was about as keen on the game as anyone I've ever met. He literally couldn't get enough golf. The morning after the match he dragged my cousin Jack out of bed to squeeze in another 18 holes before heading off to Liverpool to catch the boat back to South Africa. While chatting after their game together, Jack remarked: "Young fella you've got

tremendous talent, but you'll never do any good hooking the ball like that." In fact, Bobby carried on hooking it exactly like that for the rest of his life and it worked rather well! But while Jack's advice on the swing didn't make a lasting impression, his gift of a pair of white golf shoes did. Bobby never forgot that gesture and after the war would insist that Jack join him for one of his practice rounds at the Open. I loved this because I used to get in on the act, too.

One thing you could safely say about Bobby was that he had a unique swing. He had a very weak grip and aimed a mile right, so at the top of the backswing his club was pointing virtually at right angles to the target with the face very open. He would start his downswing with an

exaggerated turning of the shoulders and upper body which looped the club outside his backswing plane. The thing was, he aimed so far right in the first place that the club was still swinging down from inside the target line and thus every shot started right with a draw-flight. All through his career he drove with an old-fashioned brassie – ie. a two-wood – with the No.1 stamped on the sole. Whenever we played in exhibition matches there would be shouts from Bobby of "back on the right, please." He would then fizz his drives past their noses and the ball would obediently draw back to the middle of the fairway. It was like he could cast a spell on the ball.

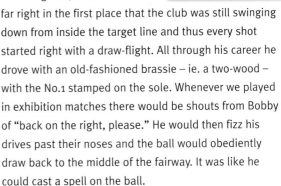

His iron play was unbelievable, too. Again he drew every shot, but whereas most hook shots tend to roll, Bobby's stopped quickly since he hit down on the ball with his huge shoulder roll as opposed to the wrist roll employed by most golfers who hook the ball. He was a wonderful judge of distance. I remember we were tied for second playing the last hole together in a tournament at Sunningdale in the early 1960s. After good drives, I hit my approach shot bang on line and he slightly over-hooked his to the left of the pin. I thought "I might have him here" but when we got to the green I was short and he was pin high and inside me! It was uncanny how often Bobby was exactly pin high. I holed my putt and he followed me in from 20 feet. That was typical of Bobby, too.

His swing was so repetitive, as I am sure were his swing thoughts, which explains how he could play so well with so little practice. I'm not kidding, he would amble on to the range to hit a few six-irons, a couple of drivers and a few wedges. Then on the way to the first tee he'd casually stroke a couple of putts. That was him ready for action. He never seemed to play badly. Oh, now and then he'd hit a shot that started right and didn't draw back as far as he intended, but I'm talking small margins. He was just incredible. Sam Snead at the height of his powers was induced to play a series of exhibition matches against Bobby in South Africa and was trounced. Weeks later Bobby turned up on the US tour, where most unsuspecting pros took a dim view of his portly physique and loopy swing and didn't rate his chances. Snead knew better and being one who liked a bet, especially one with the odds stacked in his favour, backed Bobby to do well. Bobby duly obliged and won the season's money list the first time of asking and Snead won a fortune in bets. In just over two seasons he played in 59 tournaments, won 13, was second in 10 and third in seven. Sadly, Bobby was in a car hit by a train at a level crossing, sustaining serious injuries which cut short his winning career when he was still only in his early forties.

I played a lot of golf with Bobby over the years and he really was the complete golfer, to my mind perhaps the most underrated of the century. He was a very accurate driver, a great iron player, spectacular putter and brilliant strategist who knew when to attack and when to play safe. Even under pressure he had such a clear mind and was always supremely confident. And he was always a real pleasure to play with.

21: Locke's key to natural putting

DIAGNOSIS: Bobby Locke was one of the great putters of all time, with a unique style that could take you by surprise when you saw it for the first time. He aimed right, his stance distinctly closed. He would then draw the putter back on the inside and in the throughswing loop the club outside the line of his backswing by turning his shoulders into the ball. It was highly unorthodox but everything moved together as one unit. There was no independent hand and wrist action, which made it very repeatable. I promise you he never putted badly, it was unbelievable. He was also a phenomenal reader of putts who used to concentrate particularly on a radius of about three feet around the hole, as that was where the ball was travelling relatively slowly and thus at the mercy of even the subtlest of borrows. It worked like a dream. I lost count of the number of times I thought he was going to miss a putt, but the fact that his putts were always the correct weight meant the ball often fell in the side door entrance to the hole.

EXPLANATION: Bobby's putting stroke was like a miniature version of his full swing. It had all the same characteristics – backswing inside the line, with the downswing outside the line of the backswing but still from the inside as the body turned through. Today on the professional tours, many putters rock the shoulders to keep the putter swinging straight back and through. Bobby was different. He turned his shoulders to hit from the inside to straight through. He claimed he modelled his stroke on that of Walter Hagen, who was another great putter, but I'd have to say it's not a method I'd recommend in its entirety to anyone else. Nevertheless there are certain snippets that I believe we can all draw inspiration from.

Bobby Locke had a very unusual putting stroke, in as much that he aimed right and turned his upper body into the ball as he swung the putter down and through. It's not a method I could recommend to the club golfer, but everyone would benefit from observing the way all the moving parts in Bobby's putting stroke complemented one another.

CORRECTION: In my experience, most players have a putting stroke which replicates their full swing tendencies and let me say now that if you have found a method that works, don't change it.

What is important for every golfer to understand, though, is that the correct combination of clubface alignment and swing path is the key to success. Bobby Locke repeatedly used a stroke which applied the putter face slightly closed at impact on a very slight in-to-out path. Conversely, a few fine putters cut their putts using an out-to-in path through the ball with an open face at impact. The strokes could not be more different, yet they each set the ball off on the correct line, consistently. That is the crux of the matter. Even if you choose not to make a stroke that produces a perfectly on line, square clubface at impact, so long as the face and path complement one another – as it did in Bobby's stroke – then the ball will travel on the line you intend it. Therefore you should

concentrate on other key factors such as committing yourself to the line of the putt and the length of backswing which allows a rhythmical acceleration through the ball to achieve the correct distance.

Also bear in mind that your own character and temperament can influence what sort of putter you become. If you are a laid-back person by nature, someone who goes through life at an easy pace, then you will probably be more of a Bobby Locke type of putter who thinks distance is all important and thus likes to roll putts at a dead-weight. On the other hand, if you are a more upbeat, aggressive person then you'll perhaps be more comfortable putting in the style of a Gary Player or a Tiger Woods, someone who likes to give long putts a run and who has the courage to minimize the break of short putts by striking them at speed. Make up your mind which of these contrasting styles is more your style and let that be the basis of your whole strategy on the greens.

Speed determines the amount of break you play on a putt. If you like to hit your putts firmly, or you putt mostly on slow greens, the ball will not be severely affected by the slope on its way to the hole (right). However, if you like to die your putts into the hole at a slow speed as Bobby did throughout his career, or you putt on slick greens, then you'll have to play a lot more break (far right).

Sandy Lyle

Alexander Walter Barr Lyle. The Scottish ancestry is obvious in his full name, even if the distinctly English country-boy accent suggests otherwise. But by the time he'd become one of Europe's finest golfers, Sandy was the name and magnificent ball-striking was his game.

During an interview at the age of 16, young Sandy was asked by a local newspaper reporter what he'd like to have achieved in 10 years time. "I'll expect to have won the Open," he replied. The fact he went on to fulfil that dream at Sandwich in 1985, albeit one year behind schedule, was a continuation of the inexorable and impressive progress he had been making since the age of three when he first whacked a ball nearly 100 yards. Born the son of a Scottish teaching pro, Sandy was playing golf before he was knee-high to a one-iron and by his early teens was every bit the amateur sensation of his generation. He grew up bigger and stronger than

everyone else and hit it further than everyone else. He simply dominated every level of competition that came his way. At the age of 14 he was hitting 600 balls a day, every day, a regime that paid off with his first cap as a boy international. At 17 he was the best amateur in the country, winning the English Amateur Strokeplay by a shot, courtesy of a birdie, birdie, par finish. That performance earmarked him as a born winner and I'll never forget Michael Bonallack, a great amateur and a shrewd judge of talent, hinting to me that Sandy was one to watch.

Anyone taking that advice literally in the years that followed would have been taken on a roller-coaster ride of emotions – awe at the manner of Sandy's ball-striking,

which was nothing less than magnificent; disbelief at the prodigious distances he would hit his famed one-iron; admiration for the phlegmatic way he went about his business; and every now and then frustration at the wild shots that once in a while blighted his game even when he was winning tournaments. This was part of Sandy's charm, though, super-human and yet somehow more fallible than other golfers of his class.

I was thrilled when asked to have a look at his swing during the build up to the 1988 World Matchplay Championship. His distinctive inside-the-line takeaway had become a little too pronounced, so I took him to the second hole on the East Course at Wentworth and there on the side of the teeing ground placed a ball at least 10 inches below the level of his feet. He said: "I can't hit shots from there," but I said: "Trust me Sandy, just go ahead and hit one." He couldn't take the club back too far on the inside because the teeing ground was in the way, so he was forced to swing the club back straighter which put his swing more on plane. It was a simple but effective exercise that any flat swinger would do well to rehearse. Anyway, I went off to Spain the next day to do some coaching and when I came back to London on the Monday morning I picked up a newspaper and saw that Sandy had won the title. He had made a point of mentioning the lesson I gave him, which was typical of Sandy – such a lovely, likeable fellow.

Earlier that year he had become the first Briton ever to win the Masters and for my money his bunker shot on the last hole shares the award for Shot of the Century with Gene Sarazen's stroke of genius on the par-five 15th more than 50 years earlier. I know one is often reminded during the Masters coverage of the 'flattening' effect the television cameras have on Augusta's contours, but I do feel it's worth highlighting again how steep the lip of that bunker is on the 18th fairway. The imperious manner in which he clipped a seven-iron 165 yards up on to the green was deeply impressive, a pin-sharp snap-shot of the man's phenomenal talent and also his ability to play the 'big shots' well. His unflappable nature enabled him to do things like that all through the 1980s, but beneath his laid back demeanour lurked a mean competitor and a real fighter. I think in the 1990s he lost some of his meanness, along with a bit of confidence. He also lost the ability to consistently roll three shots into two. I remember when he was at his best he was a great 'up-and-downer' but somehow he became the sort of player who when he made half a mistake, tended to drop a whole shot.

But let's not dwell on his shortcomings. The fact is, if ever I'm at a tournament I never miss the opportunity to watch him hit long irons on the practice ground – it's a magnificent sight. I can honestly say that Sandy is one of the most gifted ball-strikers I've ever seen. It's so disappointing that his particular brand of magic seems to have evaporated. His many friends, which most certainly includes me, would be so delighted if he could regain the confidence so necessary for success.

22: Play your short shots with an open clubface

DIAGNOSIS: Sandy's whole game has been built around hitting the ball with a slightly open clubface. As anyone who has seen him play will know, he takes the club back very much on the inside, but he balances this by fanning open the clubface. He then comes over the top slightly in the downswing, still with the clubface open which means he hits a kind of pull-fade. He is unbelievably strong and at his best it was wonderful to watch him blast his one-iron down the left side of the fairway before bringing it back into the middle with a touch of fade. He was like Ben Hogan in the sense that the open clubface enabled him to aim down the left side without any fear of hitting a hook.

Although his swing has never been entirely orthodox, it is extremely well-balanced in that all the moving parts complement one another. Sandy's problem shot, the push, occurred when he tried to hit from the inside, which upset the balance in his swing because he still swung with an open clubface and that produced the most enormous push-fades. You need a lot of golf course on your right to get away with that one and it's a shot that I recall cost him the 1980 World Matchplay title when he lost on the 18th to Greg Norman by hitting it into the trees on the right.

An open clubface was also a feature of Sandy's short game. The main point I want to make to you is that an open clubface is marvellous for the short shots because you tend to hit slightly out-to-in, which promotes ball-first contact. It's also particularly effective from tight lies and

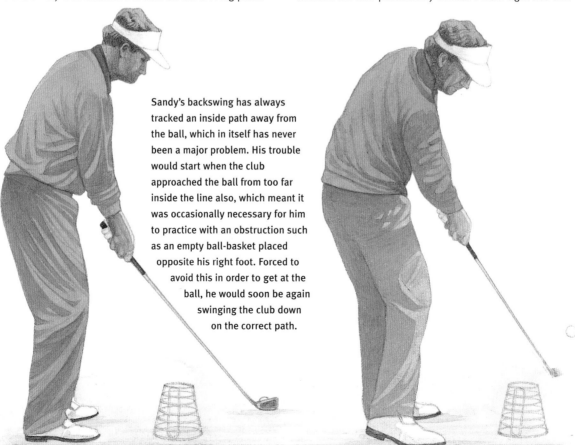

Sandy's backswing has always tracked an inside path away from the ball, which in itself has never been a major problem. His trouble would start when the club approached the ball from too far inside the line also, which meant it was occasionally necessary for him to practice with an obstruction such as an empty ball-basket placed opposite his right foot. Forced to avoid this in order to get at the ball, he would soon be again swinging the club down on the correct path.

on long bunker shots, because there's no danger of swinging into the ball on a shallow angle of attack and catching the shot fat. In that respect, Sandy's swing was tailor-made for his famous bunker shot on the last hole of the 1988 Masters.

EXPLANATION: Everybody can pitch and chip when there's plenty of room. The advantage for someone who plays with an open clubface is that they can play the really delicate shots just as easily as the straightforward ones. Sandy was like that. He was such a good chipper because his shots would have a kind of floating trajectory, the ball always landing ever-so-softly. He was also a great putter, a factor which tends to get overlooked when one thinks of Sandy's golf game.

CORRECTION: Let's deal with the two key elements of Sandy's short game – the descending angle of attack and the open clubface. On any short shot the angle of attack is the most important of the four impact factors, because that is what determines the quality of strike. Mis-hits

occur when a golfer tries to help the ball into the air and the clubhead reaches the bottom of its swing arc before it reaches the ball – the result being either a duff or a thin.

What you have to understand is that in order to make the ball travel upwards, you have to swing the club downwards. A good swing thought is to try to finish with the clubhead low to the ground when you play a regular chip shot. This encourages the correct, slightly descending, angle of attack and keeps your hands ahead of the clubhead – a combination that helps eliminate the danger of you scooping at the ball.

If that swing thought isn't enough, here's a useful pitching drill that you can work on during a practice session. It involves placing a second ball roughly eight inches behind the object ball. To avoid contact with the second ball, the clubhead must travel into impact on the correct, descending angle of attack. If you combine that with a slightly open clubface and keep the body moving, thus avoiding independent hand and wrist action, you'll learn to hit wonderful soft-landing pitch shots. I guarantee it.

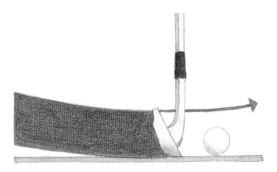

The angle of attack is crucial on chip shots because it determines the quality of strike.

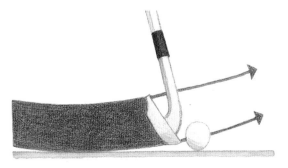

Mis-hits occur when golfers try to help the ball into the air and the clubhead 'bottoms-out' before it reaches the ball.

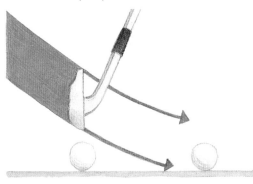

To encourage the correct, descending angle of attack, place a ball roughly eight inches behind the object ball.

In order to avoid the second ball you are forced to swing the club down, which produces a crisp strike.

Colin Montgomerie

Colin ended the 1980s with an 11-shot maiden victory in the Portuguese Open and ended the 1990s as Europe's most consistently impressive golfer, with a string of Order of Merit titles to his name. Seldom has a golfer made such impressive and relentless progress up the golfing ladder.

Consistency could be Colin Montgomerie's middle name, for it has been the hallmark of his career ever since he won the Scottish Amateur Championship in 1987 and followed that up with a rookie of the year performance in his first full season on tour. His performance thereafter in Europe is astonishing, so for the record here is the run down of Colin's finishing position in the money list between 1989 and 1998 – 25, 14, 4, 3, 1, 1, 1, 1, 1, 1. The kind of golf that buys you a cool £6 million in prize money.

That he hasn't taken a backward step is an accurate reflection on the consistency of Colin's entire game, his overall strength being that he has no real weaknesses. Off the tee he is deceptively long, his drives launched with a piercing trajectory and a faithful hint of fade. His iron play clearly prospers from the fact that he plays so many times from the short grass and, for a big chap, he really does have a lovely touch around the greens. Relative to the rest of his game one might say his putting is the poor relation, but it never

strikes me as being quite as bad as he often suggests and once a few putts start to drop he seems quick to capitalize on the upturn in confidence and thus is a very impressive putter when he is 'on a roll'.

Colin was born and educated in Scotland and brought up in a golf-mad family – indeed his father

eventually became the secretary at Royal Troon Golf Club. It was inevitable I suppose that Colin should have his hands on some plastic golf clubs as early as the age of one, but very fortunate nine years later to meet professional Bill Ferguson, a fine teacher who would guide him to the top. Bill once said of Colin's game: "He is a natural player who never had anything drastically wrong." Natural is the crucial word there. Colin's swing has no discernible differences today to the youth who first stood out in the Walker Cup matches of 1985 and 1987. As a result, he has so much faith in his swing that he gets by on less practice than any other player of his calibre. He plays by feel, not by numbers. Colin himself once said: "I've never had to work at it – the game of golf has come easily, which has been very handy."

What doesn't come easily to Colin, though, is an unflappable nature. He is too easily wound up by comments or distractions in the gallery, when the virtues of a blind eye and a deaf ear would serve him better. Just like everyone else, he is prone to missing the occasional short putt. But his problem isn't so much that he misses them, rather his reaction to missing them. At times he lets frustration get to him straight away and I think he struggles to put it behind him, so he'll tend to have a bad round or even a bad tournament just because of a couple of missed putts.

This isn't to say I don't understand Colin. Indeed, I have every sympathy for him, because nothing has annoyed me more in my life than my own golf. When you are desperate to do well and you want something so badly, it can be difficult to accept one's own mistakes. As I said earlier, if I had my time again I would definitely seek out a sports psychologist. Perhaps this would help Colin's cause. When I think back to the majority of golfers who

get to his level, they are aided by a great temperament, yet this is sometimes the weakest 'club' in Colin's bag. If he learnt to harness his considerable intelligence to more positive effect on the golf course, there would be no stopping him.

It's unfortunate that Colin didn't get a lucky break in one of the many majors he contended earlier in his career, such as the US Open at Pebble Beach in 1992 and at Oakmont in 1994, because if he had I think he would have started the new millennium with possibly three or four majors tucked under his belt. I can remember saying to Tony Jacklin, "Win a major while you're young, because with every year that goes by it gets harder to win your first." Tony achieved that, of course, and went on to prove my 'follow-up' theory by winning a second major less than a year after his first. Can Colin win one? Well he's a marvellous player and he has the game, no question about that. But can he develop the temperament? I hope so, but only time will tell. I get the feeling, though, that if he wins one he'll go on to win at least another.

23: Shape your drives to increase your margin for error

DIAGNOSIS: There are very few better drivers of the ball than Colin. He's a longer-than-average hitter, with an impressive, piercing trajectory. But more importantly he's an accurate hitter. This accuracy off the tee stems from Colin's ability to cultivate a particular shape of shot – namely, the fade – and trust that shot implicitly on the golf course. He usually aims down the left and ever-so-slightly fades the ball into the middle of the fairway. The only time I have ever seen him struggle off the tee was in the early part of 1998 when he decided he wanted to draw the ball. This shot has its merits, but it went against Colin's natural way of playing the game and thus he was for a while uncharacteristically inconsistent. When he went back to his trusty fade he started driving the ball wonderfully again.

EXPLANATION: Colin's tee shot strategy is a great way of playing because it eliminates half of the danger on a golf course. Think about someone who aims straight down the middle of the fairway. They only have to stray off line by half the width of the fairway to finish in the rough either side. Now look at Colin's strategy. He aims down the left side and fades the ball. If all goes according to plan, the ball finishes in the middle of the fairway. If the ball flies dead-straight, he's in the left half of the fairway. And if he over-cuts it he's in the right half of the fairway. Colin's margin for error is twice the width of someone who aims down the middle with no particular shape in mind.

CORRECTION: Bobby Locke used the same theory but applied it with a draw. Whether you favour this shot or Colin's is largely irrelevant. What you must simply do is think about your game and identify a shape of shot which you prefer and which best suits your swing. Call it your stock shot. Work on grooving that shape and learn to trust it and stick with it. That's playing to your strengths, something all good players do.

By having a shape of shot he can trust, Colin can aim left safe in the knowledge that the ball will most likely fade into the centre of the fairway.

24: Hit 'em quick

DIAGNOSIS: The defining feature of Colin's putting stroke is the pronounced way he strikes the ball on the upswing. This is a product of his distinctive method. He aims a hair left of centre, controls the movement with a rocking of the shoulders and then hits up on the ball with the clubface opening through the ball. You could say it's like a miniature version of his full swing.

EXPLANATION: Colin's putting stroke creates a lovely roll on the ball, but for many I believe it's a more difficult way of putting compared to, say, the sweeping inside-to-straight through method of Ben Crenshaw which we covered on pages 24–25. Besides, Colin's way of putting is only really effective on slick greens. It is also what I would describe as a 'high maintenance' method in as much as for most people it requires a lot of practice to keep it running efficiently.

CORRECTION: I would hesitate in recommending Colin's method to anyone who doesn't already find it a very natural way of putting. However, getting away from the technical side for a moment, one of the things I really do like about Colin's putting stroke is the no-nonsense way he gets on with it. Once he's over the ball and is committed to the line it's 'one look, bang'. No hanging about. I think that's a good way to putt, mainly because the longer you stand over a putt the more chance you have to tense up or talk yourself out of holing it. Next time you have a few spare minutes, go on to the practice putting green and give Colin's 'one look and hit' method a try. Make up your mind on the line before you are over the ball – and I mean really commit yourself 100 per cent to that line. Then once you're over the ball, see the line and hit the ball along it. Strike a good putt and leave the rest in the lap of the Gods. You can do no more than that.

One final thing. Under no circumstance should you ever deviate from that routine. Many times I see people take twice as long over a crucial putt, which usually means they don't hole it. Look back to the penultimate hole of the 1997 US Open, when the gallery distracted Colin as he was about to putt. Now that wasn't Colin's fault, but it knocked him out of his usual routine and in my view that's why he missed the putt. So try to stick to your routine at all costs. You'll putt better for it, I promise you.

Once Colin has chosen his line and settled over the ball, it's simply 'one look and hit'.

Byron Nelson

To most people Byron Nelson is known for the greatest winning streak in the history of golf – 11 consecutive tournament wins and 18 in one season. A quite staggering accomplishment. For my money, he also stands out as one of the true gentlemen of the game.

If anyone ever tries to tell you that you have to be mean to be a winner and that nice guys don't make champions, just say the name Byron Nelson. Here is absolutely the most charming man you could ever wish to meet, who also happens to be one the most successful golfers of all time. Along with Ben Hogan and Sam Snead, he was part of another Great Triumvirate – the third such trio of the 20th century.

I had the pleasure of Byron's company in one of the most wonderful weeks of my golfing life. The year was 1955 and along with Bernard Hunt, Peter Alliss, Tony Harmon and John Pritchard (who was later tragically killed

in a car accident with the great amateur Philip Scrutton) I'd gone over to play on the US winter circuit. John and I arrived early for The Thunderbird Classic in Palm Springs, having failed to make the cut in the previous week's event. What a blessing in disguise that turned out to be. When we went to practice at The Thunderbird Club, we happened to meet up with Byron Nelson who invited us to practice with him. We played together three days in a row.

Although he'd retired from competitive golf by then, he was still only 38 and a wonderful player. A tall man, with a classic upright golf swing, one of the things that stood out about his game was that he hit every shot absolutely dead-straight. Not a hint of a draw, or a fade,

just arrow straight which I thought was very uncharacteristic for a great player, but at the same time very impressive.

I didn't see Byron again until 1967 when each of us was doing some television commentary during the Open Championship at Hoylake. One day when we were sitting down having a chat, we got on to the subject of Byron's swing. I'd read his book *Winning Golf* which led me to believe that he'd started out with a very rounded golf swing – which he confirmed, adding that: "I could win with that swing, but I could miss the cut with that swing, too." He told me that in 1944 he took six months off to work on changing his grip and learning how to take the club straight back into a more upright backswing, quite a challenge for someone who had swung the club around himself for 15 years. The changes transformed him into a truly great player. I'll never forget how he summed it up to me that day at Hoylake. He said, and I promise these were his exact words: "I knew I would never play badly again." There was nothing conceited about that remark – Byron just knew he was right.

He wasn't kidding, either. The following year, 1945, he won 11 straight tournaments and 18 in total. I've looked many times at his record that year and frankly it still amazes me the scores he shot. Sceptics say, "Oh the fields were weak in those days." Nonsense! What they conveniently overlook is that Nelson's stroke average that year was 68.33. That's better than any leading stroke average on the US Tour since. His fourth round stroke average was even better than that, 67.68. And remember, this was 1945. His winnings for the season amounted to more than $60,000, which was nearly 15 per cent of the total purses available that year. Put into perspective, someone would need to win nearly $18 million on the US

Tour in today's money to match Byron's achievement.

After that, aged 34, he retired from tournament golf, although he did win the 1955 French Open while on holiday with his wife. Along with Bobby Jones, Byron achieved something that few sportsmen in history have been able to – quit while they were ahead. His own explanation was simple and typically honest: "I was just tired," he said. "Tired of the travel, tired of the notoriety, tired of having to find new goals."

He had a point, of course. Where do you go after winning 18 tournaments in a single season? In Byron's case, to his beloved ranch near Fort Worth in Texas which he had bought with some of the prize money from that epic season. He never disappeared from the world of golf, though. For much of the seventies and eighties he was Tom Watson's mentor and coach, applying his knowledge and experience to help shape a marvellous golf swing that picked-up five Open Championships. To this day he retains his position as honorary starter at the Masters, a role he held until 1999 with the late Gene Sarazen and Sam Snead. He is also the only professional golfer to have a named tournament on the US Tour, the Byron Nelson Classic. It's probably about the only thing he hasn't won – although the trophy still has his name on it!

25: If you swing too flat, Byron's your model golfer

DIAGNOSIS: Byron Nelson was another golfer who went from good to great by changing his swing mid-way through his career. Like Hogan, he was a winner of major tournaments and therefore hugely successful, but he knew there was more talent in him that his current technique was stifling. He was proved right.

Byron was a tall man and his theory was that a more upright swing might suit him better and, more crucially, help keep the clubhead on line for longer through the hitting area so he wouldn't have the tendency to hit the occasional shot to the right. His swing became very straight, not dissimilar in many ways to Jack Nicklaus' action. He adopted a weak left-hand grip, with the back of the left hand square to the target, and pushed the club straight back away from the ball very much with his left arm and shoulder controlling the swing. It was a left-side dominated movement all the way to the top of the backswing, followed by a pronounced leg-drive and dip of the head as he swung the club down into impact. This distinctive movement re-established the arc of his swing and helped prevent his angle of attack getting too steep.

EXPLANATION: I believe that every golfer who picks up a golf club sees the swing in either one of two ways. Some will picture the golf swing as being very much straight-up-and-down the play line, such as Byron Nelson or Colin Montgomerie, and these golfers will have a tendency to fade the ball. Others see it as

Note how Byron's left arm is on a very much more upright plane than the shoulders – being a tall man this suited him perfectly, whereas golfers of a shorter stature tend to do better with a more rounded action.

being a more rotary movement, such as Ian Woosnam, and these players will tend to draw the ball. When I'm teaching people I automatically pick up just from the first couple of shots how that person sees the swing – straight or rotary. The problems start when you become either too straight or too rotary. Or put another way, too upright or too flat.

CORRECTION: If you have a golf swing that is too flat, then you would be well-advized to follow Byron's lead in changing to a more upright action. Practice moving the club back on a straighter line in the takeaway, using predominantly your left arm and shoulder to control the movement. The key is to make sure your right shoulder moves behind you as the club swings up. This prevents your shoulders rocking in sympathy with the straight-back arm-swing, a fault that will cause your swing to become excessively steep and narrow. I would also advize practicing from a lie where the ball is below your feet. This encourages the hands and arms to swing higher in the backswing, in order to reach the bottom of the ball.

If on the other hand your swing is already too upright, then you need to focus on introducing a little more body turn in your backswing, rather than taking the club straight back and upwards with your arms. In other words, a more rotary action. This is best achieved by practicing with the ball positioned on a sidehill lie, the ball above the level of your feet, and then concentrating on the correct shoulder turn.

It's all about getting the correct balance. Let me remind you that in golf you must turn your body because the ball is to the side of you, but you must also swing the arms up because the ball is on the ground. It is OK for one to be slightly more pronounced than the other – for instance, Byron was more arm-swing than body-turn, Ian Woosnam vice versa – but you mustn't let one element completely dominate the other. That is when you will start to have problems.

Jack Nicklaus

To be dominant at any one time is a monumental achievement. But to dominate across several decades, meeting and beating generations of opponents is simply staggering. Yet that is precisely what Jack Nicklaus achieved – seeing off the world's best players in the sixties, seventies and even the eighties.

Few sportsmen in history have dared even to think, let alone proclaim, they were the greatest of all time. Muhammad Ali thought it, and frequently said as much, but let's face it he was probably right. Jack Nicklaus could never have been as outspoken as Ali – that just wasn't his style. But although he never said it, in his heyday big Jack surely knew he was the greatest and his peers knew it to.

You could almost see the effect that Jack had on opponents. His mere presence on a leaderboard would cause most golfers within shouting distance to crumble, their self-belief shrivelled by the thought of the Golden Bear on their tail. In addition to his intimidating persona, Jack had more power up his cashmere sleeve than any other player, an almost super-human talent for concentration and a level of composure that suggested ice ran through his veins. Kipling's words, "if you can keep your head, while all around others are losing theirs..." obviously weren't written for Nicklaus, but they might as well have been, because Jack could always play his own, remarkable game when the pressure was at its most intense, when other players simply could not.

Jack was setting records virtually from the day he took up golf aged 10. At 13 he was down to a handicap of plus-three. Three years later he got to play with Sam Snead in a friendly match and, inspired by the old pro's rhythm, went out the next week and won the Ohio State Open, beating some very useful professionals with his already mature and strong all-round game. The speed and momentum of his development as a golfer was like a runaway

train. While still an amateur, he led the US Open with only six holes to play, eventually pipped by the king himself, Arnold Palmer.

Jack didn't have to wait long for his first major victory – the 1962 US Open – clearly enjoying it so much that every year thereafter he seemed to be able to peak for the 'big four'. When he started dominating The Masters, a tournament he went on to win six times, its founder Bobby Jones remarked that "he plays a game with which I am not familiar." And he was right. Nicklaus used to hit the ball prodigious distances in his youth, with equipment that looks positively stone-age compared to the space-age materials used now. Recalling his victory in the 1965 Masters, when he shot an eight-under par 64, Nicklaus says: "...that round of golf was like walking down Main Street. It was nothing. I'm hitting nine-irons and wedges and everyone else is back there with three-irons. I'm sort of laughing and snickering and saying 'Boy this is a tough golf course, huh.'" People raved about Tiger Woods at Augusta in 1997, but they forget Jack was doing that 30-odd years ago.

This power game, allied to his iron will and a scary reputation, gave Jack the greatest Major record in history – six Masters, five USPGAs, four US Opens and three Open Championships – a feat I personally don't think will ever be beaten. No other golfer has won each major more than once – Jack has won them all at least three times! It's not just the 18 wins, though. Jack also registered 46 top-three finishes in major championships and 73 top-10s.

Five times in his career Jack managed to win more than one major in a calendar year. He

was also the leading money winner on the US Tour a staggering eight times.

There is much, much more – but alas one would need an entire book in order to cram in his achievements. Quite simply, Nicklaus is the greatest. If there is any doubt, let some of his contemporaries, and other legends of the game, have the final say. Asked in 1995 who he thought was the greatest player of all time, Arnold Palmer said succinctly: "I think Nicklaus would have to be given that nod." Gary Player simply says: "The greatest scorer that ever lived was Jack Nicklaus." Gene Sarazen remarked in 1975 that "Nicklaus is the greatest tournament player we have ever had." Tom Watson said in 1982 that he "is the greatest player in the history of the game." These are the most telling testimonies.

The Jacobs' defence rests its case.

26: Keep your chin up

DIAGNOSIS: For me personally, Jack is the greatest player the game has ever known and yet as a ball-striker he is vulnerable to elementary technical flaws, just as you and I are. I remember back in the 1969 Open at Lytham, I walked to the second tee and there was Jack playing a practice round with Gary Player and Gardner Dickinson. The first drive I saw him hit went miles right over the adjacent railway line. So he reloaded and then hit the biggest pull hook you've ever seen, practically killing someone standing on another fairway. He did the same at the third. I walked with the three of them to the sixth, a big par-five, where Jack again got out his driver and hit another drive at least 50 yards off the fairway on the right. Jack turned to me and said: "You're supposed to know a bit about the golf swing, what do you think about that?" Well, I'd heard both Gary and Gardner telling him for the first six holes to get his backswing more rounded as opposed to very upright.

But as I said to Jack: "You can't possibly get your backswing more rounded with the posture you've got." Jack said: "What do you mean posture?" I replied, "The back of your neck is actually parallel to the ground." His chin was so buried in his chest that he could only tilt his shoulders. There was no room to turn.

EXPLANATION: It doesn't matter who you are – Jack Nicklaus or Joe Soap – a fault like this at address will lead to difficulties in the swing. Letting the chin drop upsets your whole posture, ruining those all-important angles that are created in the upper body and making a good shoulder turn impossible. When the shoulders 'rock' in the backswing, the body 'blocks' in the downswing. Jack always described this as 'rock and block'.

Jack's chin had a tendency to drop a little too low at address, which made it difficult for him to turn his shoulders correctly in the backswing.

CORRECTION: My suggestion to Jack was simple but effective. It would be the same advice I would give to any golfer who came to see me with a similar fault in their game. I said to him: "Doesn't anyone ever talk posture to you, Jack?" He looked at me and actually said, "Well funnily enough every time Jack Grout [Nicklaus' long-term coach] sees me hit shots he pretends to give me an upper-cut to keep my chin up." I suggested to him that he better start doing that pretty quickly, so we stood on that tee for about 15 minutes and hit at least a dozen drives.

This time Jack kept his chin up and his back much taller. That was all it took. Jack started to make a more effective upper-body coil, because there was room to turn his shoulders correctly. As soon as he started to make a

better rotation, the plane of his backswing returned to normal, which meant his left side now cleared in the through swing, allowing the hands and arms to swing the club through as opposed to being blocked.

After that, virtually every time I saw Jack he would say to me: "John, have you got a minute to check my address position?" It's a pleasure to work with someone like Jack, of course, but there was one occasion when I had to turn him down. It was later that same year at the Ryder Cup at Birkdale when Jack arrived in the car park the same time as me. In front of dozens of people he said: "Hey John, I'll see you on the practice ground in half-an-hour." I said to him: "Jack I dare not be seen teaching you on the eve of a Ryder Cup match. Can you imagine the fuss?" Fortunately he understood.

As soon as he kept his chin up, it made room for the shoulders to turn more correctly and lead to a better rotation – not only in the backswing, but also in the downswing which meant his left side cleared allowing the hands and arms to deliver the clubhead to the back of the ball with his customary authority.

27: Jack's pre-shot routine – nobody did it better

DIAGNOSIS: There are so many superlatives one can attach to Jack Nicklaus. Perhaps the least spectacular, but most significant, are his methodical approach and incredible powers of concentration. To me, the two go hand in hand. Jack left nothing to chance. I don't think his pre-shot routine changed one little bit in all the years that I watched him. That in my opinion is one of the reasons why he could stand up in the most pressurized situations and hit not just great shots, but winning shots. His pre-shot routine helped him concentrate to such a level that mentally each shot was much like any other.

EXPLANATION: Think about a shot you've seen Jack Nicklaus hit – any shot. You can probably picture in your mind his exact routine – over the years it's been as predictable as a Swiss watch. Lining up the shot from behind the ball, aiming the clubface over an intermediate target between the ball and the flag, settling very steadily into his address position ... finally, a couple of slow waggles and then the familiar swing and intense look of concentration as his eyes follow the ball's often radar-like progress towards the target. Jack never hurried, he never let anything get in the way of his routine. Every time he stood over the ball, he was 100 per cent ready to hit that shot.

CORRECTION: I think Jack summed up brilliantly the value of a pre-shot routine when he said: "Give your imagination free reign when you're in a position to win and it can be the death of you." He is referring to the fact that if you let your mind wander, especially into the future, you're in big trouble. A pre-shot routine stops this happening. It crystallizes your thoughts and help focus the mind on the things that are relevant to that shot, to the exclusion of everything else. Most amateur golfers have no real pre-shot routine. My advice to you now is develop a consistent way of building up to hit a shot. It doesn't need to be exactly the same as Jack's, but I think it should incorporate certain elements from the great man.

Firstly, picture the shot in your mind's-eye, from behind the line of play. This gets you mentally 'into your shot' so you're thinking positively and constructively. Next, aim the clubface over an intermediate target between the ball and

Jack's pre-shot routine is a marvellous example of how to focus 100 per cent on the job at hand. He always looks down the target from behind the ball, visualizing a mental image of the ball's flight.

the flag. It's far easier to aim at something a couple of feet in front of you than a flag 250 yards away – and if the gun is aimed correctly, you have a much better chance of hitting your target. Also, be very specific about what you aim at. This is relatively easy when the flag is your target. But when you're driving off the tee, never aim just anywhere down the middle, because in my view if you aim vaguely you swing vaguely, too – and that's when you're prone to making stupid mistakes. Finally, have a couple of waggles of the clubhead. It relieves tension in the hands and arms, which spreads through your body and helps

you make a smooth, unhurried backswing.

Work hard on perfecting your pre-shot routine when you're at the driving range. This is the place where you develop the good habits which enable you to perform to a higher level in competition. Nobody ever practiced as well as Jack did. Every ball he hit on the range is treated the same as the second shot to the last hole of a major championship. In my opinion, amateur golfers hit too many shots on the range with too little thought. Try to get into the mind-set of hitting less balls with more thought. Quality, not quantity – that's what practicing is all about.

He then aims the clubface over an intermediate mark, such as an old divot, between the ball and his target. For some this is much easier than trying to aim at something perhaps as far as 250 yards away.

Jack then builds his stance around the clubface alignment and once he is settled makes a couple of slow, methodical waggles of the clubhead. This helps keep tension out of his hands, arms and shoulders.

Greg Norman

Nobody lives a fuller, faster life than Greg Norman. Business tycoon away from the golf course, while on it his unrivalled combination of great athleticism, physical strength, aggressive nature and strong character make him a constantly exciting and formidable presence.

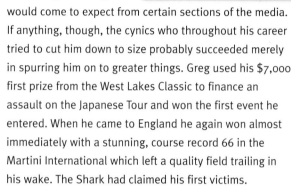

Some players have won more tournaments than Greg Norman. Some have won more majors, too. But few can pull in a crowd like Greg Norman, amass a fortune like Greg Norman, astutely manage a billion-dollar business like Greg Norman, attract endorsements like Greg Norman, attack golf courses like Greg Norman, risk life and limb in daring off-course escapades like Greg Norman, own half-a-dozen Ferrari's like Greg Norman and illuminate rooms with his mere presence like Greg Norman. He is, by any stretch of the imagination, a man of many considerable talents.

This much was obvious from an early age. Greg didn't start playing golf until he was 15 and on the advice of the

local club professional "hit it as hard as you got" made sufficiently speedy progress to get down to scratch within two years. Phenomenal energy levels and a huge appetite for success, qualities that have never deserted him, supported a punishing practice regime and within a couple more years he had won his first professional tournament, the West Lakes Classic in Australia.

He was a virtual unknown, not even a full time member of the tour, but smashed the course record by three shots in the first round, outshone seasoned pros such as David Graham and Bruce Crampton and made headlines with his prodigious hitting, reducing par-fours to a drive and a chip. One local newspaper described his sensationally-long drives as "downright insolence," an inane criticism if

ever I heard one, but something that Greg would come to expect from certain sections of the media. If anything, though, the cynics who throughout his career tried to cut him down to size probably succeeded merely in spurring him on to greater things. Greg used his $7,000 first prize from the West Lakes Classic to finance an assault on the Japanese Tour and won the first event he entered. When he came to England he again won almost immediately with a stunning, course record 66 in the Martini International which left a quality field trailing in his wake. The Shark had claimed his first victims.

In the late 1970s Greg and Seve were the two most talented golfers that I had ever seen emerge at the same time. One blond, one dark, the pair could not have been more contrasting to look at, yet they shared an on-course presence that was simply electrifying. Greg's game was all about power. When he stepped on to the first tee you felt he had one purpose in mind, to grab a golf course by the scruff of the neck and batter it senseless. He was a disciple of Jack Nicklaus having learnt the game from Jack's instruction books. Although highly effective, Jack's swing was by no means perfect and in following his style to the letter, Greg inherited the same mistakes. He asked my opinion on his swing at the Dunlop Masters in the early 1980s and what I saw was a straight, rock and block golf swing that generated so much lateral leg slide in the downswing that his spiked right shoe couldn't hold its ground. Like Jack, Greg was so talented he didn't let swing flaws get in the way of him winning. Nevertheless, I think he has a lot to be grateful to Butch Harmon for. Although they parted company in the late 1990s, I believe Butch got him swinging the club a lot better, encouraging him to turn more correctly over a stable leg action.

Old swing or new swing, Greg has been one of the

longest straight drivers of the ball the game has ever known. He is flat-out, pedal-to-the-metal aggression and when he gets it right he is awesome. Remember the 64 in the final round of the 1993 Open at Sandwich, or the 63 on the way to winning the 1986 Open at Turnberry? You won't see better rounds of golf than that. The trouble was, the strength and aggression that made Greg such an exciting player also meant that his mistakes were often of the 'crash and burn' variety. People said he was a choker, but I disagree. Greg had the temperament to win. But he had a flawed technique that occasionally stopped him winning. And, of course, he was on the receiving end of some outrageous strokes of fortune. Whichever way you look at it, the sheer number of near-misses in Greg's career reflect the fact he was in contention more than anyone else – in the line of fire, so to speak – and that is a tribute to his game. He may not have won as many majors as his remarkable talent once promised, but I admire him for the way he's played the game and for my money he is certainly one of the top 20 golfers of the century.

28: Hover the club to promote a more correct shoulder turn

DIAGNOSIS: One distinctive feature of Greg's game is how he hovers the clubhead of his driver above the ground at address. It is one of the things that he picked up from a Jack Nicklaus instruction book. So why, you might ask, does he do that?

EXPLANATION: Well, Greg claims that it keeps tension out of his hands and arms, which promotes a smooth, wide one-piece takeaway and good overall rhythm in the swing. That makes sense. He also says it enables him to maintain a constant grip pressure, removing the tendency to re-grip the club at address. Again, sound advice since a lot of club golfers have a habit of re-gripping which can not only result in grip flaws but also upset the clubface alignment before your swing has even started.

CORRECTION: While I would go along with Greg on those points, I think hovering the clubhead at address has another very important benefit. For those who tend to tilt their shoulders in the backswing rather than turn, which Greg did for many years, hovering the clubhead off the ground helps you turn more correctly. The reason for this is it encourages you to stand a little bit taller at address, rather than hunch over the ball, and that improvement in posture helps promote a better turn. Remember, when you turn your shoulders in the backswing there is a degree of tilt brought about by a slight tilt in the spine angle at address. But if you hunch over the ball too much, there is too much tilt in the spine angle at address which converts into too much tilt in the backswing. This causes your swing to be too straight.

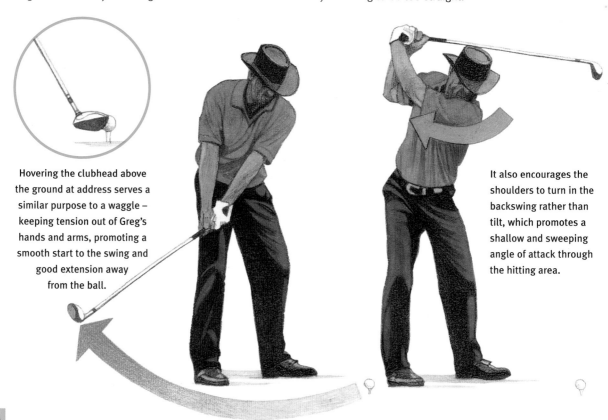

Hovering the clubhead above the ground at address serves a similar purpose to a waggle – keeping tension out of Greg's hands and arms, promoting a smooth start to the swing and good extension away from the ball.

It also encourages the shoulders to turn in the backswing rather than tilt, which promotes a shallow and sweeping angle of attack through the hitting area.

29: Show some commitment

DIAGNOSIS: One of the many things I like about Greg's game is his unflinching commitment to every shot he hits. No half-measures, no pussy-footing around. When Greg makes up his mind about a shot you can be certain he will give it 100 per cent. It's true with his driving, where he uses every ounce of power in his muscular and athletic frame to smash the ball down the fairway. And it's true in his short game, especially his putting where he holes out with such conviction and commitment.

EXPLANATION: When I think of Greg hitting one of his signature, power-house drives, I'm reminded of Peter Thomson's description of his swing. He once said it was "like a stretched bow. You draw back the string and, foom, let the arrow go." That I think conjures up the level of commitment in Greg's swing – he really doesn't hold back, he lets the ball fly and accepts the outcome, good or bad.

CORRECTION: It would be easy for me to glibly say to you that you need 100 per cent commitment on every shot. While this is undeniably the truth, the fact is you can only truly commit yourself to a shot that you actually believe you can play. This is why it is so important to make on-course decisions based on the limitations of your own game. Greg's ability knows virtually no bounds, therefore he can approach pretty much every shot he looks at with a high degree of self-belief, confidence and commitment. But even the Greg Normans of this world know when to back off and play safe.

When you are playing a competitive round of golf (by all means feel free to experiment when there is nothing on the line) you must also learn to appreciate the value of selecting shots that are appropriate to your capabilities. In some situations such as tee shots there is not much of a decision to make, other than club selection, and thus it is easier to be committed to the shot. But in all other areas you must be brutally honest with yourself and choose shots that match your ability rather than your aspirations. Only then will you be able to benefit – and believe me, you will benefit – from the kind of committed approach that makes Greg such a great player. You'll also avoid the total disaster holes that can so often be the wrecking of any round.

Greg's no-holding back approach makes him one of golf's most dynamic drivers.

Mark O'Meara

Like a fine claret, Mark O'Meara has improved with age. As a young man he was obviously a good player, but it was only when he turned 40 that he fulfilled his true potential. The two major championship wins in 1998 merely confirmed his status as a mature, well-balanced golfer very much of the Premier Cru.

I've watched Mark's steady but impressive progress in the game with great interest ever since I first saw him on the practice ground at the Open Championship in 1981. I was teaching a few of the players of the day and he wanted me to have a look at his swing. No tour professional could have been more of a 'rocker and blocker' than Mark was then. We worked together for an hour or so to try to encourage a more correct turn, less of a tilt. I then recommended him to a teacher in the States who worked for me at that time, Hank Haney. Next time I

saw him was at the Open at Sandwich in 1985. Mark was now pretty orthodox and it was kind of him to remind me of my suggestion for him to visit Hank. However, when I saw him again at Troon in 1989 his swing had actually become a little flat. His turn was correct but the arm-swing was not up enough – the complete opposite of eight years previously at Sandwich.

Today and for many years now he has swung the club very well, whereby both the body action and the co-ordinated hand and arm action have been spot on. It was no surprise to me at all when he suddenly won two majors. You couldn't wish to see a more correct or simple motion. Indeed, Mark has one of those swings where as a

viewer you're always surprised when the ball doesn't go exactly where he intends it.

As a youngster he took a while to find his feet in the game, but he broke through in the best possible way when he won the 1979 US Amateur, giving the defending champion and now fellow tour pro John Cook a right old-fashioned stuffing 8&7. That glorious triumph lined him up for a date with embarrassment, though. Playing the Masters with the previous year's winner Fuzzy Zoeller, as is the custom for the Amateur champion, O'Meara shot a first round 81. "It was a long, long day," he recalls. I don't suppose that experience exactly filled him with confidence for his date at the US Open with another defending champion, Hale Irwin, so perhaps in hindsight it isn't surprising that Mark again struggled, only just breaking 80 in both rounds.

But sometimes the harshest lessons in life are the most valuable. Mark was a great putter and it was obvious that he had talent, but the swing he had then would have undoubtedly held him back. It is a credit to Mark that together with his coach Hank Haney he has been able to develop such an efficient and classy golf swing. Seldom is he more efficient than when he sets foot on the hallowed turf of Pebble Beach, where he has become very much the man to beat. Back in 1979 he won his first big amateur title and five times as a professional he's won the tour event they play there every year. Horses for courses, as they say. Either that or the sea air must agree with him, because it was on the links of Britain in our Open Championship that Mark most looked like winning his first major on a few occasions. But come the last few holes on a Sunday afternoon, he was never in there with a real chance of winning. Somehow, for many years he could

never quite bring his major game to the majors.

That all changed at the 1998 Masters where on the manicured lawns of Augusta National all the pieces finally fell into place. Mark drove the ball solidly, hit the notoriously unforgiving greens in the right place and in keeping with his reputation, putted like an angel all week. Having never finished in the top-three at Augusta, suddenly he was slipping on the Green Jacket.

This led to an interesting turnaround in O'Meara's thinking. When I look back at truly dominant players in history – the likes of Jack Nicklaus, Tom Watson, Arnold Palmer – they each shared one crucial characteristic, self

belief. They turned up at the major championships believing they could, and would, win. I'm sure the 1998 Masters gave Mark that all-important self-belief. So when he showed up at Birkdale later that year for the Open Championship, on a course he liked and played well on, he genuinely believed he could win. And that, more than any of the pure iron shots he hit or the smooth putts he rolled in, is why he did win. Having played in nearly 60 major championships without so-much as a runner-up spot, let alone a victory, he had all of a sudden won two in three attempts.

At the age of 41, O'Meara had finally made his mark.

30: Posture, turn and clear – three steps to swing heaven

DIAGNOSIS: I believe Mark is as good a swinger as there is in the game. But it's like looking at a different person to the one who came up to me on the practice ground at the 1981 Open. Like many young players growing up in the 1970s, I'm sure Mark's swing would have been shaped to some degree by the leading player of the day, Jack Nicklaus. While this technique brought Mark some success, it also brought much pain because that shape of swing can create a tendency to swing the club too straight, causing the body to tilt more than it turns.

EXPLANATION: Because the ball is to the side of you, the arc of the swing has to be in-to-in to some degree. It is not a straight line. Mark, like many players, used to have the perception that the straighter you swing the club the straighter you will hit the ball. That would only be true if the ball were between your feet. But readers, please digest this next sentence, the ball is to the side of you and therefore when you take up your posture you need to make room for a swing arc that travels in-to-square-to-

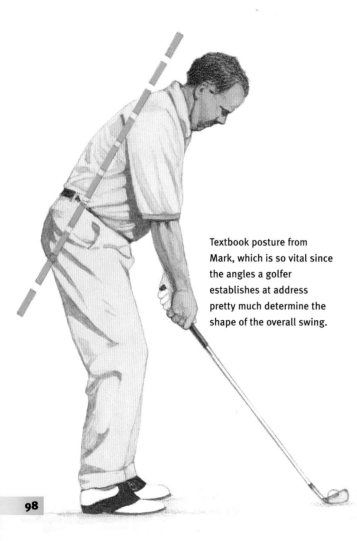

Textbook posture from Mark, which is so vital since the angles a golfer establishes at address pretty much determine the shape of the overall swing.

From such a great starting point Mark can turn his shoulders 100 per cent correctly, while swinging the club up into the perfect backswing plane.

in. Mark, just like anyone else, had to understand this before he could physically start to do it.

There is only one moment when the clubhead is on line and square, that is at impact. Not before or after. When you swing the club too straight the clubface is square until it gets to impact when it is not square. When you swing it correctly, the clubface isn't square until you get to impact with the ball, which is when you want it square.

One of the best analogies is to compare the position of the clubface in your swing to the position of your hands when you clap. Think about it, your hands are only square to one another when they meet – not before. And nobody has missed yet! It's a natural in-born timing that we all have. However, if you try to keep your hands facing each other and sweep them back and forth in a dead-straight line, it doesn't feel at all comfortable. The whole clapping motion will lack timing and

authority. This is what happens when you try to swing the golf club too straight.

CORRECTION: Teaching Mark was like teaching Jack Nicklaus – to start with it was all posture, posture, posture. Good posture at address – the key elements being slight flex in the knees, spine tilted forwards only very slightly, chin up and weight over the balls of both feet – allows you to turn your shoulders so that as the arms swing the club up, there is also room to swing the club to the inside. What Mark was doing was tilting his shoulders in the backswing so that the left shoulder was too low and the right shoulder too high. This makes the shoulder plane too steep, and the arms and club follow suit.

Let's just re-emphasize that point. Start with good posture in order to facilitate the correct body action and therefore the correct arc of swing. By turning in the backswing, you can then turn more easily in the through-swing, which means the left side is out of your way, providing plenty of room for the arms to swing from the inside and back to the inside. This in turn encourages the correct angle of attack. This all starts from correct posture. The pros work on it all the time, quite the opposite of the old hackneyed cliché 'keep the head down' and far more constructive.

Mark's spine angle remains constant from the moment he sets up to the ball to the time he swings the clubhead through impact. In maintaining his height so well he makes it easier for himself to swing the club freely into the back of the ball, without having to do any fast and fancy last-second corrections with his hands. It's a classy looking action and incredibly efficient.

Jose Maria Olazabal

Near-crippling injury halted Jose Maria Olazabal's career in its tracks. But the young Spaniard is nothing if not a real fighter. Fit again, that spark of brilliance that fuelled such success in his twenties has been reignited, ready to sustain more dazzling low scores and tournament wins throughout his thirties.

I can clearly recall the first time I met Jose Maria, or Chema as he is known. He was a precocious 13-year-old and I was doing some coaching for the Spanish Golf Federation, as I had for many years. You will expect me to say that Chema stood out from the crowd, but I must confess that at the time he didn't strike me as being anything particularly special. He was just one of many very talented youngsters in the Spanish youth side.

Looking back it was obvious he had determination and ambition. Also, the foundations of an exquisite short game were pretty much evident. I'm sure this was in part due to the fact that as a three-year old he had practiced his putting and chipping on the course his father tended to as greenkeeper, San Sebastian in Spain. The course actually opened on the day Chema was born – 5 February 1966 – and it is touching that this toddler should have used it to develop the phenomenal short-game skills he demonstrates for real on today's world stage.

Chema wasn't just one of the crowd for long, though. By his early teens he was a scratch golfer and before he was out of his teens he had won the unprecedented triple of British Boys' Championship, the Youths' Championship and the Amateur Championship, handing Colin Montgomerie a drubbing in the final. Naturally, it was around this time that everyone started to realize he had something special and that he had the necessary temperament to be a star of the future. He didn't flatter to deceive. When he turned professional he developed virtually overnight into one of Europe's premier golfers. He qualified for the first Ryder Cup he was eligible for and alongside Seve Ballesteros went on to form one of the most dynamic, successful partnerships in history. He was also winning tournaments all over the globe, including the 1990 World Series of Golf where an astonishing 11-under par 61 set him up for an impressive 12 shot victory against a class field. All this and he was still only 24, remember.

During this time we really didn't see much of each other. Then in 1992 we were at Wentworth together doing some promotional work. It was the week after he'd taken a bogey-five at the last to lose the Masters by a shot to Ian Woosnam and he was very depressed about it. I remember saying to him: "Come on, Chema, you didn't play very well last week and you still finished second. That's how good you are." He appreciated what I was saying, and I think he agreed, but it took him a long time to get over that loss and it seemed to drag his golf game into a kind of mini-slump.

More than a year later, in the build up to the 1993 Ryder Cup at The Belfry, I noticed he still wasn't playing very well. I was having a chat with the captain Bernard Gallacher, who has been a great friend of mine for many years, and I asked him to let Chema know that if he wanted to I'd come up to The Belfry and take a look at his swing. Chema took me up on the offer and I met him on the practice ground. What I saw shocked me. His swing was all wrong. The ball was too far back in his stance, the club was too strong, which meant he tilted his body in the backswing and got in the way of himself in the downswing. I coaxed him back into good shape fairly quickly, as you will find out in the lesson on the next page, and he played pretty well that week. A chance meeting in Spain in February 1994 helped give him more confidence, which gathered momentum and culminated in a fantastic performance that won him the 1994 Masters and he followed that up almost immediately with a win at Wentworth in the PGA Championship.

Just as he was riding high, of course, he was forced to pull out of the 1995 Ryder Cup through injury to his feet. He had an operation, but the benefits were short-lived and the problem returned, only this time far worse. "It wasn't a question of whether he would play golf again," said his manager Sergio Gomez, "but more a case of whether he would ever walk again." At near-desperation point, Chema was introduced to a controversial specialist who thankfully diagnosed the problem and within weeks the doctor's treatments began to work. He then proved what a true champion he is by winning in only his third tournament back from a 12-month layoff.

We still work together from time to time and I still see in him that burning desire to be the best. I must say I think he is too hard on himself when he feels he isn't playing to the best of his ability. But when he gets it right he really is as good as anyone. You only had to be sitting in front of the television watching the 1999 Masters to appreciate that. What a composed and magnificent performance that was.

31: Ball forward produces a knock on effect

DIAGNOSIS: As I've said, I clearly remember teaching the young Chema when I used to fly out to Spain to coach the Spanish national amateur teams. I've taught him on and off ever since and, as is so often the case, the faults he had in his swing way back then still have a cruel habit of creeping into his game to this day. Double US Masters winner or not, old habits die hard.

What happens is the ball sometimes drifts further and further back in his stance at address, which feels natural to him but it has a terrible knock-on effect on his golf swing. The worst I'd ever seen this was in the lead up to the 1993 Ryder Cup at the Belfry.

EXPLANATION: With the ball too far back in the stance every iron club in the bag has a 'false' loft on it – the five-iron is like a three-iron, the seven-iron is like a five-iron, and so on – and I don't need to expand on the difficulties that can create with regards to judging distance and flighting shots correctly. But that's only the start. Having the ball too far back puts the right side too high at address and the left shoulder too low. This made Chema, as it would any other golfer, lean on to his left side, which causes the shoulders to tilt rather than turn in the

backswing and this creates an excessively steep swing plane. Golf being the chain reaction that it is, the weight unfortunately tends to stay too centred, even drifting towards a reverse pivot.

All of this made it very difficult to attack the ball from the correct inside-the-line path. Chema was having real difficulty hitting the ball squarely and solidly, especially with the longer clubs such as the driver.

Correct ball position also promotes good weight transfer and encourages the shoulders to turn into a more powerful position at the top of the backswing.

Placing the ball correctly opposite the left heel is essential for the longer clubs in the bag, especially the driver. It sets your upper body 'behind the ball' at address and establishes the appropriate tilt in the shoulders – the right noticeably lower than the left.

CORRECTION: On the practice ground Chema needs a fair bit of convincing to make the necessary change. But as soon as he put the ball further forward in his stance, the difference in his swing was night and day. It raised his left shoulder into a more natural position and also set the clubface into a more neutral position behind the ball, with just the amount of loft that the club manufacturer intended. From here, he can turn his shoulders correctly. This positioned his body, and the club, perfectly at the top of the swing, which made it easier for him to unwind his body more correctly in the downswing. All of these improvements are reflected in the quality of his impact position. The body is more willing to clear out of the way, providing free passage for the arms to continue swinging down and through. And the ball is now in the right position for the swinging clubhead, enabling Chema to strike the ball with his customary authority.

Like many others, Chema is fine on the practice ground but less confident on the golf course. He has such a great short game, as was in evidence at Augusta in 1999, and is such a fierce competitor that he is a great player even when not at his best.

This good work in the backswing enables you to unwind the body correctly in the downswing, providing free passage for the hands and arms to swing the club dynamically through impact on the optimum path for power. And with the ball being ideally placed in the stance, the clubhead meets it on the ideal angle of attack. It all adds up to the perfect recipe for long, straight driving.

103

Arnold Palmer

Here is the only golfer who ever had his own army – Arnie's Army. For a whole generation he was golf's first real hero, a swashbuckling, power-house player whose entire philosophy on a golf course was to "hit it hard, go find it, and hit it hard again."

Arnold Palmer was quite simply golf's most exciting player, ever. In terms of his style of play, he well-and-truly broke the mould. Whereas the likes of Hogan, Snead, Nelson and all the other dominant players of the forties and fifties possessed classic, stylish swings, along came Arnie slashing at the ball with those strong hands and Popeye forearms, charging around like he was picking a fight with every tee, fairway and green. He wasn't interested in plotting his way carefully around a golf course, he wanted to batter it into submission. I'm bound to exaggerate, but looking back it seemed to me that Arnold had two ways of playing a hole, either smash it down the middle, knock it on the green and drain a long putt; or carve it into the trees, murder it out of the rough, chip on and slam-in the putt. His roller-coaster style of play and distinctive good looks drew enormous crowds, whipped-up a frenzy of media interest and brought vast sums of money into the game, boosting tournament purses and ushering in a new era of 'big-bucks' player endorsements. Every one of today's mega-rich golfers should tip their logoed visors in Arnold's direction and thank him for the extra zeros that appear at the bottom of their cheques.

Arnold learnt how to play golf from his father, who was the greenkeeper and professional at Latrobe Country Club in Pennsylvania. Hit it as hard as you can, then learn to hit it straight, was his father's advice, a policy that Arnold followed to the letter. Surprisingly for such a great player, Arnold was an amateur right up until the age of 25

and was only convinced he could make a living at the game when he won the US Amateur in 1954. But with a $5,000-a-year contract from Wilson under his belt, he soon made up for lost time. Within 12 months of joining the tour Arnold had won his first tournament. And when he came over to play in the 1960 Open at St Andrews, he'd already won a couple of majors and was just about the dominant player. Although he finished runner-up to Kel Nagle that week, his mere presence gave the kiss of life to a tournament that had lost some of its clout on the world scene. Suddenly everyone wanted to come over for the Open. I got to know him soon afterwards and I must say I liked him straight away and have done ever since. He's a good, honest man and, despite his superstar status, I think very normal and down-to-earth.

As soon as Arnold swapped his street shoes for spikes, all sense of normality disappeared. Watching him in his heyday was the most compelling of sights. There was nothing scientific about Arnold's swing – it relied on one thing ... power, and lots of it. Arnold was built like a middleweight boxer and gave the ball a fearful crunch. I'm not kidding, the earth practically shook when he hit the ball. I'll never forget a great story from when Arnold was playing in the final round of the 1964 Masters with Dave Marr, a witty and charming man who sadly died in 1998. Arnold torpedoed one of his awesome long-iron shots towards the water-guarded 15th green, shooting straight into a low sun. Blinded by the light, he looked to Marr and enquired: "Did it get over," to which Marr memorably replied: "Hell Arnold, your divot got over!" Laying up never was Arnie's style.

For all his power, though, Arnold's chipping and putting was what made him a champion. He used to hole no end of long putts. We all used to think he was a lucky

blighter, but the putts kept going in so it was nothing to do with luck! Even Jack Nicklaus said: "Arnie at his best was the greatest chipper and putter I've ever seen."

To me, the 1960 US Open sums up Arnie's career in a nutshell. He'd had a poor first three rounds, which left him well off the pace going into the final round. All week Arnold had tried and failed to drive the green at the 346-yard first hole, but predicted that if he could knock it on this time he "would shoot one hell of a score. Maybe even a 65." At 1.45pm that afternoon, Arnold plucked the driver out of his bag, smashed his ball on to the green and two-putted for a birdie. He then went birdie, birdie, birdie, par, birdie, birdie. Arnie was on a charge and his Army went

bananas. His championship-winning 65 that day is one of the greatest rounds in history. It is also significant for being the tournament where for the first and last time three legends would compete – Hogan in his last serious shot at a major, Palmer the King of Golf, and Nicklaus the young crew-cut pretender to the throne. It was a fascinating battle, which Arnold won in typical fashion – from behind, charging along with his faithful Army in tow.

He won eight majors in all, but it's almost an insult to talk of Arnold's career in terms of statistics. He changed the whole face of the game. Watching him play badly was more entertaining than watching most other golfers play well. The game of golf has a lot to thank him for.

32: Stay still and give your putts a rap

DIAGNOSIS: Arnold was the boldest putter I've ever seen. He charged his putts at the hole, without a second thought for the one coming back. He was just so confident. There was a real sense of acceleration through the ball. It's one of the reasons Arnold holed so many long putts in his career – the ball was struck so firmly that it fought to hold its line all the way to the hole.

EXPLANATION: Arnold's putting stroke wasn't only positive, it was also perfectly timed. There was a wonderful rhythm to it. People talk about rhythm in the full swing, but it's just as important with the putter. The putter should flow back and forth, smoothly but with good rhythm and acceleration through the ball.

CORRECTION: Good rhythm in your putting stroke stems from the correct length backswing. If the backswing is too short, you have to really hit at the ball to create sufficient speed. If your backswing is too long, you have to decelerate to avoid hitting the ball too hard. Work at developing a length of backswing that enables you to swing the putter into the back of the ball with natural acceleration. Your stroke should feel positive and purposeful, but at the same time very rhythmical. As you make practice putting strokes try to feel the length of swing that will send the ball the required distance. Then repeat that stroke and let the ball get in the way of the swinging putter-head. If your stroke is smooth and rhythmical, I promise you will be surprised how quickly your judgement of pace improves.

Arnold's putting stroke had wonderful rhythm to it, the putter-head always meeting the ball with a real sense of acceleration. Lagging putts was definitely not his style.

33: Be careful what you copy

DIAGNOSIS: Many people are surprised when I say Arnold was not a great driver of the ball in his heyday. But that was indeed the case. He was long, but he could also be wild and part of the reason for that was the flat left wrist at the top of his backswing. He became a great driver by gradually getting his left wrist into a more orthodox, more upright position at the top. Virtually every year I used to see him he would say to me: "It's getting better," referring to the work he was putting in on this aspect of his game.

EXPLANATION: Ben Hogan once said: "Arnold's swing might work for him, but no one else should try it." He was right. Arnold played brilliantly almost in spite of his technique. As with even the greatest players, only certain elements of their game are applicable to the club golfer. Identifying these is what this book is all about.

CORRECTION: There aren't many golfers in the world who could play well from a position at the top of the backswing like Arnold's. The arched left wrist would put the clubface so shut there wouldn't be a golf course wide enough to accommodate the wild pull hooks and pushes. Take a minute to check the position of your left wrist at the top of your backswing. You don't want a flat, or arched left wrist. Instead, upright with even a degree of 'cup'. That's more neutral and it allows you to swing the club down more freely and on the correct path into the back of the ball. I find this arched and hence shut clubface at the top is usually caused by the shaft of the club pointing to the left of target at the top of the backswing. If you practice consciously pointing the club in the direction of the target at the top, this invariably improves the hand and wrist position at this crucial stage of the swing.

One element of Arnold's game that I do suggest you copy is his grip. He had one of the best looking grips in the game. It looked like his hands were born to hold a golf club, which wasn't far from the truth because his father taught him the correct grip from the age of three – albeit at that age his grip would have been relatively strong, then modified as he grew up. If you mould your hands around the grip as Arnold did, there's a tendency for a lot of good swing traits to stem from that.

No harm could come of copying Arnold's grip, though. His immensely powerful hands looked like they were made for holding a golf club.

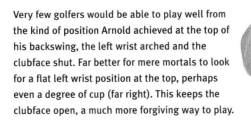

Very few golfers would be able to play well from the kind of position Arnold achieved at the top of his backswing, the left wrist arched and the clubface shut. Far better for mere mortals to look for a flat left wrist position at the top, perhaps even a degree of cup (far right). This keeps the clubface open, a much more forgiving way to play.

Gary Player

Often dressed in black, as if perhaps to mourn the impending defeat of his opponents, Gary Player called upon almost super-human levels of guts and determination throughout his career to become one of the most prolific winners the game has ever known. To my mind he is also one of golf's greatest ever characters.

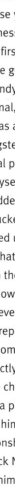

It brings a smile to my face when I think of the young, crew-cut Gary Player first coming over to Great Britain and I can remember vividly the first time I ever played golf with him. It was during the week of the Open Championship at St Andrews in 1955 and I was on the tee with John Fallon, a fine British player. We were just about to start a practice round, when on to the tee walked this young kid and he said: "Excuse me Mr Jacobs and Mr Fallon, could I join you?" Naturally, we agreed.

Gary would have been just 19 years old at the time and, though I'm sure many readers will be surprised to learn of this, had a really poor technique. His grip was incredibly weak and his backswing was very flat. He hit every shot with a pronounced hook. But it was uncannily repetitive and he had a magical short game. There was something about the teenage Gary Player, I promise you, which smacked of something special. Greatness shone out of him.

After that first practice round at St Andrews we quickly became good friends. Gary used to stay with a family near Sandy Lodge in Hertfordshire, where I was the club professional, and he occasionally came there to practice. He was an amazing character. Still is, of course. But as a youngster he was tremendous fun, always laughing. A real practical joker. I remember walking along the Champs Elysees in Paris with him in the middle of the day and he suddenly shouted at the top of his voice "Look out!" We all ducked, but there was nothing happening. When we looked up he was creased-up laughing. He was always doing that sort of thing, absolutely mad. If we were driving in the car to a tournament he'd often wind-down the window and yell out to passers by. "Straight-on, is it?" They'd never have a clue what he was talking about, but invariably replied 'yes', much to Gary's amusement! He was great company, always has been ever since. His father was exactly the same, a lovely man and a real larger-than-life character.

And what a player Gary has been. I have enormous admiration for him. When you consider that he won nine major championships spanning 30 years, despite his two great rivals, Jack Nicklaus and Arnold Palmer, being both stronger than him and longer off the tee. Not to mention the fact that he chose to travel backwards and forwards from his home in South Africa, clocking up more air miles than Biggles!

Together, Gary, Jack and Arnold were another Great

Triumvirate. Rather like Vardon, Braid and Taylor, they all played the game very differently but could each get the job done when it mattered. In many ways I've always felt that Gary epitomized my classic 'identikit image' of a champion. The most important ingredient of all is temperament – it is the uppermost characteristic of any great champion. Second on the list is technique and third is strength. That's Gary Player for you. Yes, he practiced harder than anyone to improve his swing. And yes, he trained like a prize-fighter to build up his strength and fitness. But it was always going to be his temperament, the sheer guts and determination of the man, that made him a real winner.

There's little doubt in my mind that to Gary, golf was as much a battle of wills as any clinical examination of physical skills. It is why he excelled so marvellously in head-to-head encounters, winning five World Matchplay titles and once coming back from seven down at lunch to beat the stylish and highly gifted American Tony Lema.

But the format of the game mattered not to Gary – matchplay, strokeplay, any play, he simply loved winning. You could see it in the way he played the game and by heavens you could always see it in his trademark punch-the-air, victory celebration. Maybe this is another reason why he became so adept at finishing first.

On top of all those wonderful tournament victories, he even pipped his great rival Jack Nicklaus to membership of golf's most exclusive club – joining Ben Hogan and Gene Sarazen as a winner of all four major championships. For more than 40 years, this relatively small South African has been a true giant on golf's world stage. He's a remarkable individual.

34: Let a blade of grass point to a better grip

DIAGNOSIS: Gary Player used to say, and indeed still does say, that the harder he practiced the luckier he became. Maybe so, but there comes a time when practice in itself is not enough. Every golfer needs pointers from time to time, even if it is only the tiniest of swing thoughts, to get them back on the right track.

When I look back on the young, fiery, competitive Gary Player, apart from the talent oozing out of every pore I can also remember the faults that would plague his game every now and then. The worst, and most persistent of these was the hook – a damaging shot, even if you're one of the so-called 'Big Three' of the 1960s. Gary was always fighting off the tendency to hit the occasional hook, especially with his driver and long irons. There are many causes of this shot, but Gary's main problem was that he tended to release the club too early in the downswing – in other words, cast the clubhead. The clubhead was basically travelling too fast for Gary's leg and hip action.

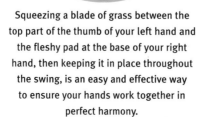

Squeezing a blade of grass between the top part of the thumb of your left hand and the fleshy pad at the base of your right hand, then keeping it in place throughout the swing, is an easy and effective way to ensure your hands work together in perfect harmony.

EXPLANATION: Because Gary's hands and arms were so active so early in the downswing, the club basically reached the bottom of its swing arc too soon, before it even reached the ball. So the shot would start to the right simply because the club was travelling in that direction having failed to reach the on-line portion of its swing arc, which as I said was due to the hips being left behind.

The ball then curved left in the air because the hands and arms, still working ahead of everything else, closed the clubface too early through impact. That's a recipe for the hook – and that's what Gary and thousands of other amateurs over the years have struggled to cure.

CORRECTION: In my experience, casting of the club from the top is often caused because the hands have started to work independently of one another. So I gave Gary a tip that would encourage his hands to work together in harmony throughout the swing – as a unit rather than against each other. It involves a prop that any golfer in the world cannot fail to lay their hands on – a single blade of grass.

I asked Gary to hit balls with a blade of grass trapped between the top of his left thumb and the palm of his right hand. Then to apply enough pressure to keep that blade of grass in place throughout the swing and to also concentrate on a more active clearing of the left hip in the downswing. This is the exercise I would prescribe to any golfer suffering from similar problems. The blade of grass helps eliminate the separation between your hands, which is causing the clubface to close and the ball to swerve left in the air. And focusing on clearing your left hip will help bring the clubhead more on line into impact and therefore get your shots starting on line. It worked for Gary Player. It should work for you, too.

35: The master of imagination

DIAGNOSIS: Gary was a fearless putter. He used to 'straighten' short putts by banging the ball firmly into the back of the hole. I've never seen anyone hole out with such commitment. You might like to give that method a try. You'll soon know if it's not for you, in which case it will have been a worthwhile exercise in establishing that you are thus more suited to dying your putts into the hole. That's the way I putted all through my career. Bobby Locke was the same.

Above all else, though, Gary is best known for his sand skills. He was a great, great bunker player. And still is for that matter. Gary learnt a lot from Norman von Nida, whom he stayed with in Australia for a couple of weeks early in his career. Norman was a fine bunker player

himself and taught Gary the touch, feel and the imagination required to become a great sand player. By the time he was at the peak of his career, Gary was in a class by himself.

EXPLANATION: One of the reasons Gary became so good from sand was the way he practiced. He used to throw handfuls of balls into a bunker and then play each one as it lay. So often we lesser mortals place balls in the sand on a perfect lie and show off our skills, but when faced with something a little unusual we're suddenly not so good. When Gary practiced it didn't matter if the ball was buried, lying perfectly or on some sort of slope, he'd just deal with it. That gave him the physical skills and, just as

Tough bunker shots held no mystery or fear for Gary, because he practiced from every conceivable type of awkward lie. It's one of the reasons he's been the undisputed master of sand throughout his career.

importantly, the wonderful imagination that often separates the great from the good.

This was the philosophy he applied to practicing every department of his game. He'd spend as much time being creative as he would being conventional. I remember when we were both playing in a tournament at Crans sur Sierre in Switzerland, each night before it got dark we used to go to the course with just a putter and a wedge and take it in turns nominating shots – the idea being to get up-and-down in a pitch and a putt. We would start out with fairly orthodox shots, then become increasingly creative as our skill and imagination cried out for greater challenges.

CORRECTION: My advice to you is practice like Gary Player used to. If you're working on your bunker play, don't set yourself up with a perfect lie every time. Chuck in a dozen or so balls and play each one as it lies.

Bear in mind that the standard greenside splash bunker shot requires a combination of an open clubface and out-to-in swing path, taking a portion of sand from under the ball without hitting the actual ball. Learn how to adapt that technique to suit different situations. In a fried-egg lie you need to take more sand and generate more force, but still play with an open clubface. If the ball is completely plugged, you need a steep angle of attack and a square clubface. On any kind of slope you need to alter your weight distribution at address to vary the angle of attack. By giving yourself these shots to play, you soon learn how to deal with them.

And feel free to carry this varied approach right through your entire game. Ideally, get together with a friend and call different shots, just as Gary and I did. If you're on your own, call the shots yourself. This kind of practice fuels your imagination and develops your technique – together that helps take your game on to a new level.

When the ball's below the level of your feet, build yourself a solid foundation at address and then keep your head at the exact same level until you splash the clubhead into the sand.

Nick Price

When Nick Price hits shots with that quick-fire swing of his, the ball leaves the clubface like a tracer-bullet seeking out its prey. In that sense, very few players in history have been as impressive to watch.

I admire Nick tremendously as a person. He lives in the manner of someone who doesn't wish to miss a thing, cramming as much adventure into his life as possible. And not only is he one of the friendliest, most charming men you could wish to meet off the golf course, I think on the golf course he conducts himself impeccably whether in glorious victory or devastating defeat.

I admire his golf game even more. Whichever club he uses and whatever shot he hits, his swing has a speed and authority that is tremendous. In that sense, as is often the case, it reflects his personality. He's a naturally

energetic, upbeat kind of person who even delivers his words quickly. Just as you might recognize him from the voice, so the mere sound of Nick hitting shots is a give-away. You can listen to the clubface crunching the ball and know it is him. It is that distinct. Watching is more advizable, though, because he really is very impressive. His swing shares a feature of a lot of good players in that as he makes the transition from backswing to downswing, he drops the club on a distinctly flatter plane from where he rips through the ball with blistering speed. It's a veritable blur of 100 per cent efficiency and correctness.

That trademark brisk tempo has always been a factor in his swing, but not always the efficiency. Indeed, when at the age of 17 he travelled from Zimbabwe (then Rhodesia) to California for the Junior World Championship

he was what you might call a streaky player. It was one extreme or the other and, as he said himself, he could "make more birdies than bogeys on the good weeks, but on bad weeks the reverse." Fortunately that particular week was a good one and he won the title, against a field of 256 players that included John Cook and Hal Sutton. Inspiring as that victory must have been, Nick had to put his golfing aspirations on ice and go through the obligatory two-year period of National Service. When he finally turned professional, inconsistency again plagued his game and even the occasional sweet smell of success could not disguise the fact that his game was fundamentally flawed.

Cue David Leadbetter. Nick had met David in his junior golf days back home and when in 1981 he left Europe and fled to the States in search of a softer climate and a sharper golf game, their paths crossed again. Under David's guidance Nick eradicated a lot of the wasted motion in his swing and thus became a far more consistent player. But strangely enough, particularly in view of what we now know about his record, he went eight years on the US Tour without winning.

Then, like a man who suddenly finds the solution to a puzzle after years of trying, all the pieces in his golf game slotted into place. He won his first major, the 1992 USPGA and the following spring became the first man in 15 years to win three tournaments in a row on the US Tour. The next year he won the Open at Turnberry. As he so eloquently put it in his winner's speech, he had got one hand on the trophy in the 1982 Open at Troon, where a back nine stumble left the door open for Tom Watson; and one hand on the trophy in 1988 at Lytham, when he played wonderfully but was denied by an unstoppable Seve Ballesteros; but here he finally got both hands on the Claret Jug. This time he was the beneficiary of someone else's inexperience, with Jesper Parnevik failing

to look at the scoreboard and playing an ill-chosen approach to the last. Price meanwhile conjured his own stroke of genius, a monster 40-foot putt for eagle on the penultimate green. Years of toil on the practice ground seemed to repay him in one magical moment. Later that same year he won another USPGA title to make it three majors victories in nine attempts, a phenomenal strike rate in modern-day terms.

The late nineties were not so prosperous, but that wasn't down to any loss of form because Nick is one of those golfers who seems to always strike the ball magnificently. The problem is his putting, his one Achilles heel. His fast swing tempo doesn't seem to convert quite so well into his putting stroke. Of course he can be a wonderful putter, or else he would not have won so much, it's just he doesn't enjoy the consistency one would expect from a player of his class. Tour players everywhere should thank their lucky stars, because if God had given Nick a putting stroke to match his long game, his record would be even more impressive.

36: Show the ball who's boss on all of your shots

DIAGNOSIS: I'm a big fan of Nick's entire game, but for the purposes of this lesson I'm going to be very specific and focus on his pitching action. I love the way he plays these shots with not a hint of sloppiness – there's a real authority and crispness in his ball-striking. His great talent is that he manages to get the length of swing snychronized with his body movement, which allows him to accelerate into the ball with authority and yet maintain superb distance control. Therefore, whether it's a 50-yarder or a 100-yarder, he knocks the ball into the green with a sense of controlled aggression.

EXPLANATION: There have been many good players who were sharpish swingers, fast and authoritative just like Nick. Then again there have been others who were just as effective swinging at the opposite end of the tempo scale. Take Sam Snead for instance. He had a slow, syrupy-smooth swing that worked a rare form of magic on whatever shot he cared to play. Yet both Nick and Sam each possess flawless rhythm. Therefore, we can't define good rhythm merely by the actual speed of the swing. Good rhythm is a speed of swing that suits the particular type of player. It ensures that the clubhead is travelling at it's most effective speed, under control, when it meets the golf ball.

CORRECTION: In view of this, what lesson can we now draw from Nick's game? Well to my mind a successful pitching method relies on you generating a length of swing and degree of body turn which enables you to accelerate into the ball with authority, whatever distance pitch shot you are hitting. This is the single most crucial area where the club golfer can benefit from some Nick Price-like authority.

Nick's quick-fire swing is deeply impressive and with a club such as the driver there really is no better ball-flight in the game today.

From any distance under 100 yards Nick manages to produce exactly the correct length backswing, allowing him to really hit the ball quite hard and yet maintain great judgement of distance.

I suggest you try this exercise. Next time you have an opportunity to practice, go out on to the range with just your wedge and a dozen or so balls. Give yourself a comfortable distance, say 70 yards, and hit the first couple of shots with a distinctly longer swing than you would usually make. Follow that up with a couple of shots using what feels like a much shorter swing than normal. Repeat the process a couple of times. What you are looking for is a length of swing that isn't so short that you struggle to generate sufficient speed, but neither is it so long that you are afraid to hit the ball. The ideal length swing should enable you to swing down with natural acceleration, producing what feels like solid ball-turf contact and the ideal distance for the shot you are hitting.

In my experience the most common mistake is to swing too long and decelerate into the ball, but equally I've seen golfers who swing the club back so short they virtually throw themselves at the ball in order to generate sufficient power. Both are as bad as each other. What you are looking for is a happy medium and the only way to achieve that is through trial and error.

Finally, here's another great tip that you can rehearse with any club in the bag. As you start your swing begin the sentence "It is the *ball* you are hitting," and aim to strike the ball when you put the emphasis on the word ball. Really say it with conviction. All through my career whenever I felt that my timing was out I often went back to this tip and it worked a treat. It promotes a smooth swing, but more importantly one in which the focus of all your energies is channelled towards impact. Give it a try first with a practice swing. I think straightaway you'll get a feeling for what I mean.

Gene Sarazen

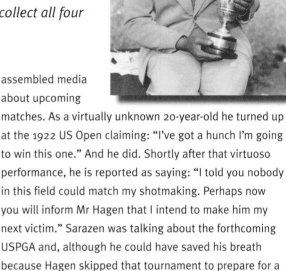

Christened Eugenio Saraceni, this carpenter's son born of Italian parents in New York, made an even more spectacular name for himself by holing the most famous wood shot in history. It won him the US Masters and made him the first man to collect all four major championship titles.

Doctor's orders, of all things, propelled Gene Sarazen down the road to golfing greatness. As a young lad he'd contracted an awful illness, which very nearly finished him off, but after a life-saving operation and a fighting recovery he was advized by his doctor to take an outdoor job because the fresh air would be good for his condition. Being a keen and talented golfer, that must have been music to his ears and he managed to secure a job in the shop at a local golf club. From that point on, destiny seemed to have a hand in writing Sarazen's script. He registered his first hole-in-one in a local tournament and noticed the following day that his name, Eugenio

Saraceni, had made it into the newspaper. "It sounded like a violin player," he recalled many years later. "So I changed it to Gene Sarazen. It sounded like a golfer."

What a golfer he turned out to be. Early in his career he had a reputation for being a relatively small man with a bigger-than-average mouth. I suppose you might say he was the golfing equivalent of Muhammad Ali, forever making bold predictions to the

assembled media about upcoming matches. As a virtually unknown 20-year-old he turned up at the 1922 US Open claiming: "I've got a hunch I'm going to win this one." And he did. Shortly after that virtuoso performance, he is reported as saying: "I told you nobody in this field could match my shotmaking. Perhaps now you will inform Mr Hagen that I intend to make him my next victim." Sarazen was talking about the forthcoming USPGA and, although he could have saved his breath because Hagen skipped that tournament to prepare for a big money exhibition match, he was true to his word and won that major, too. It was obvious that Sarazen's clubs were as eloquent as the man himself. The press loved him – he was always good for a quote.

He was really a born entertainer. I had one of the most wonderful evenings of my life in his company when in 1955 the British Ryder Cup side teamed up with a nominated American side to raise money for the Cancer Research Fund. Gene Sarazen was on their team – he was in his fifties but was still a very fine player. Sid Scott and I were going back to our rooms one night and we bumped into Sarazen in the corridor. "Come on guys," he said. "I've got a bottle of scotch in my room. Let's have a drink together." We were in Tulsa, Oklahoma and he talked about travelling that same area in the 1920s with Walter Hagen, some of his championship victories, and the big-money exhibition matches that he used to play in. For instance, in 1930 he won a then fantastic prize of $10,000 in one match in Mexico. It was fascinating stuff – a real window to the past.

He is one of the few golfers who can claim to have truly shaped the future of the game, since it was he who invented the sand-wedge. Whenever he performed in

exhibition matches he would always do his party-piece in a bunker. He was fantastic out of sand, probably as good as the professionals are at the highest level today.

Despite all the championship wins, all the great stories he told me and the fascinating tales I've read about him, the defining moment of Sarazen's career was one solitary golf shot. He'd missed the first US Masters in 1934, but the following year when he drove up Magnolia Drive at Augusta National, history was waiting for him around the corner – Amen corner. There on the par-five 15th he holed his now legendary four-wood shot. The story loses none of its fascination as the years go by. Apparently, he had a pretty poor lie and there was some discussion between him and his caddie about what club

to play. His playing partner Walter Hagen, always the joker, yelled over to him: "Hurry up and hit it, will ya. I've got a date tonight." Sarazen did hit it and, of course, saved Hagen some lost time by not needing his putter. That albatross-two got him into the playoff and he beat Craig Wood the next day to become the first man to complete golf's Grand Slam.

Perhaps to the modern generation, the name Gene Sarazen was synonymous with the honorary starter's role at the Masters, which he held until his death in 1999. But no tribute can really do justice to this man's achievements. He may have been only 5ft 4in, but Sarazen's small, co-respondent golf shoes left a giant impression on golf courses all over the world.

37: Bunker play – the easiest shot in golf

DIAGNOSIS: Sarazen was a trained pilot and got the idea for his sand-wedge from the way the flaps on the wings of a plane angled downwards to force the plane upwards. He also claimed inspiration from watching ducks land on water, the way their rounded bellies skimmed across the surface. His subsequent design of a club with a rounded sole, or flange, made the clubhead bounce through the sand rather than dig into it.

EXPLANATION: Sarazen was as orthodox as you could get in sand. Like all really good bunker players, the action of the clubhead through the sand was just like skimming pebbles across the sea. We've all done that as children, I'm sure. Just like the pebble skimming across the water, the clubhead of the sand-wedge doesn't dig down into the sand, it merely skids through the sand under the ball. That's why the clubhead is rounded.

CORRECTION: I'll apologize now because I know how annoying it can be when you hear a golf professional say how easy bunker shots are. But it is true. For one thing, the club is designed to help you. The rounded sole will slide through the sand if you let it. More than this, the margin for error is huge compared to other shots. You can hit anywhere between one and four inches behind the ball and produce an acceptable result. You can't afford to be anywhere near that inaccurate with a fairway wood or iron shot.

If you suffer from a lack of confidence with bunker shots, I recommend you practice in the sand without a ball. Open the clubface and make long, smoothly accelerating swings, getting used to the sensation of the clubhead sliding through the sand, not digging into it. If you can repeat that action when there's a ball lying there, Sarazen's clever clubhead design will do the rest for you. You'll never fear bunker shots again.

Thanks to Gene's clever invention, the sand-wedge, bunker play is the most forgiving shot in golf. You can hit the sand anywhere between one and four inches behind the ball and still produce an acceptable result.

38: Manipulate the face to create extra clubs

DIAGNOSIS: That famous four-wood shot of Sarazen's highlights one of the secrets of the shotmaker's art, manipulating the face position at address to make the club work harder for you. All great players can do this. Sarazen's ball was sitting down on the 15th fairway at Augusta. His three-wood would have produced the necessary distance to carry the lake fronting the green, but the clubhead was too large to sit flush behind the badly-lying ball. His four-wood had the right-size clubhead, but didn't offer the yardage, so Sarazen needed to improvize in order to produce the desired shot. He opted for the four-wood, which sat nicely behind the ball, and strengthened the loft on the club to squeeze out those extra yards to the green. A stroke of genius.

EXPLANATION: When the ball is sitting down it is essential to have a steeper angle of attack. Anything shallow will hit the ground before the ball. Sarazen positioned the ball back in his stance which strengthened the loft on the club to obtain the desired angle of attack and achieve the necessary distance. Under different circumstances he might have chosen to put the ball forward, weakened the club's loft and swung on an out-to-in arc to again get the desired steeper angle of attack. This would produce a higher, softer trajectory, but most probably would not have achieved the distance Sarazen was looking for on that occasion.

Gene had to hood the clubface of his four-wood to generate the extra yards to carry the lake in front of Augusta's 15th green because he was 'between clubs'. It was a shot that took courage and commitment, but the reward made it worthwhile.

CORRECTION: Golf is essentially ball control, which often necessitates changes of clubface position, swing path and angle of attack to get the desired result. These aren't things you try for the first time in the middle of a competition. That would probably end in tears. Make sure you practice it first. Experiment with different lies, different clubface and ball positions. You shouldn't feel like you have to change your swing. The club does the work for you. That's the beauty of this technique.

Sam Snead

Slammin' Sam Snead was a poor boy from a farmer's family who developed a golf swing that was like a Rolls Royce engine. Silky smooth, quiet, powerful and purposeful. It didn't matter how many miles Sam put on the clock, his swing never seemed to miss a beat.

Sam Snead, Byron Nelson and Ben Hogan were born within four months of each other in 1912 and later succeeded in continuing golf's 20th Century trend for producing a trio of great players – a Great Triumvirate – who together would dominate the game. While Nelson's career was relatively brief and spectacular, and Hogan's consisted of two 10-year spells of dominance either side of a shocking car crash, Snead's brilliance seemed to march on and on with the inevitability and momentum of Old Father Time itself.

No other golfer lasted quite as well as Snead. At the age of 62 he almost won the 1974 USPGA Championship, pipped only by Lee Trevino and Jack Nicklaus, two golfers who weren't even born when Snead was winning his umpteenth tour event! Only weeks before he'd finished runner-up in the Los Angeles Open, one of the biggest tournaments on the US Tour. He's still the oldest golfer to win a main tour event – the Greater Greensboro Open aged 52 – and for 20 years it was virtually front page news when he didn't break his age. For the record he shot a round of 60 at the age of 71 and aged 84 was still a good enough player to put together a score of 66. That is nothing short of miraculous.

Snead's talent for shooting low scores first turned heads when he got paired with a couple of former US Open champions for a round at his home club. He was an unknown assistant pro at the time, but this star-in-the-making outshone his illustrious playing partners with a brilliant round of 61. Word spread and some local businessmen offered him financial backing. Within months Snead was on his way to winning more professional tournaments than any other golfer in history. Only a suspect putting stroke prevented him from winning a couple of US Opens, which would have given him the full set of majors.

I remember seeing him play for the first time and like everyone else being awe-struck by the rhythm and power of his golf swing. The club seemed to move slowly, smoothly, like hot syrup poured from a tin. And somehow the ball appeared to leave the club slowly. But it went on for ever – Sam hit it miles with that lazy-looking swing. When he and Hogan won the old Canada Cup (now known as the World Cup) at Wentworth in the 1950s, Snead drove with a three-wood all the time. His partner, Ben Hogan (what a pairing!) wouldn't let him take his driver out because Snead tended to aim right and turn into the shot, a technique which strengthens the loft of the club. That can be dangerous with a driver, which has very little loft, but was perfect for a three-wood because it virtually delivered a driver's loft to the ball at impact. He was immensely powerful. He left enormous divots in the teeing ground, probably seven or eight inches long, because he was ripping the ball with that three-wood off a low tee-peg. He was really squeezing the ball out. He drove it beautifully – a long way, too.

I can still picture one great moment during one of his practice rounds. He was on the par-five 17th at Wentworth and had hit a good drive into the middle of the fairway. He was sizing-up the blind second shot that you have on that hole and turned to his caddie and said: "Whad'ya think?" in that southern drawl of his. The caddie explained that the line was straight at a particular tree on the horizon. "One-iron?" Snead suggested. The caddie agreed. He then hit one of the most magnificent, towering long-iron shots I've ever seen. The ball never left the tree. Snead looked at his caddie and in a nonchalant kind of way just said: "Is that about it?" An understatement if ever I heard one!

He made the game look so easy that I think people used to underestimate his knowledge and awareness of the golf swing. They thought he was just a hillbilly with a lot of natural talent. Having sat with him on the *Golf Digest* so-called panel of experts in the 1960s, I can tell you he knew much more about the golf swing than people give him credit for. He used to get quite annoyed when others, thinking they were paying him a compliment, said he was the best natural player of all time. "You telling me I haven't hit as many balls as the next guy?" he would reply. I could understand what he meant because he had worked incredibly hard on his game, even though the polished article suggested it was solely a gift from above.

What a player he was. I have to say it's been a privilege to watch him over the years. Unlike his two rivals, Byron Nelson and Ben Hogan, Sam didn't need to make changes to his swing to go from 'good to great'. He was always great.

39: Aim right and clear your left side

DIAGNOSIS: Snead had the greatest rhythm of all time. He was also talked about as being the original one-piece swinger – in other words, the hands, arms and the club all swung in conjunction with the turning motion of his body. His tendency was to aim a little right of the target, followed by a wonderful turn in the backswing. His downswing was then slightly outside the plane of his backswing as he cleared his left side into impact. He really turned his body into the shot, which meant there was lots of room to swing the club freely through the ball. His body never got in the way of his arms, which can happen to golfers who don't clear their left side in the downswing.

EXPLANATION: The strong turning motion of his upper torso built up enormous centrifugal force in the downswing which was transferred out through the arms, hands and ultimately the clubhead. That's why Sam could hit it miles with so little effort.

CORRECTION: Sam's swing was the complete opposite of being too far underneath in the downswing, a dangerous position that I see in a lot of club golfers. By the term 'underneath', I mean the right shoulder is too low in the downswing, the left shoulder too high, with the hips and upper body too square at impact. The only way you can deliver the club to the ball is severely from inside the line, which with some clever hand action might result in the occasional straight hit, but mostly means a mixture of pushed drives and snap hooks. You'll have 100 yards between your bad shots. Oh dear!

If that sounds familiar, you have to learn to clear your left side in the downswing. Try to feel that you aim a little right at address, especially with the shoulders, and turn your body into the ball as you swing down. Think of your right shoulder being a little higher as you swing the club down, the left shoulder working more around and to the left. This drags the right side through and gives you more room to release the club on line through impact. This means the ball is more likely to start on line, too.

Sam Snead's swing was arguably the most stylish of all time; certainly the most enduring.

40: Soft hold promotes great rhythm

DIAGNOSIS: There were two key fundamentals at the heart of Sam's great rhythm. First, he had a wonderfully soft grip pressure. He always maintained that you should grip the club with the same pressure you'd use to hold a live bird in your hands – one of the most valuable and enduring golf lessons of all time. Secondly, Sam never tried to hit the ball too hard. Even with his driver he was never operating at more than about 80 per cent, which meant his swing would always feel under control and in perfect balance.

EXPLANATION: Sam's greatest assets are all too often the club golfer's greatest weakness. I hardly ever see a golfer who grips the club too softly – it's nearly always too tight. And whenever the driver comes out of the bag, brute force seems to be the name of the game.

These two faults combine to have a disastrous effect. If you grip the club too tight there's no way you can make a fluid, smooth start to your swing. It will probably resemble some kind of minor electric shock and it's nigh-on impossible to retrieve a good shot from a start like that. Trying to hit the ball too hard compounds the problem. Any sense of rhythm and good balance is almost certainly destroyed. As for trying to apply the clubhead to the back of the ball on the correct path and angle of attack, that becomes very much a case of hit and miss – usually the latter.

CORRECTION: Try to follow Snead's example. A soft grip will free-up the natural rhythm in your swing and introduce a sense of fluidity to your movement. And remember, the fact that the ball is positioned to the side means the arc of the swing will be through the ball from in-to-straight-to-in. Your address should make you aware that you will be going back on the inside, so swing down at the ball from the inside and clear the left side so that the club returns to the inside in the follow-through, having delivered the clubface square and on line at impact.

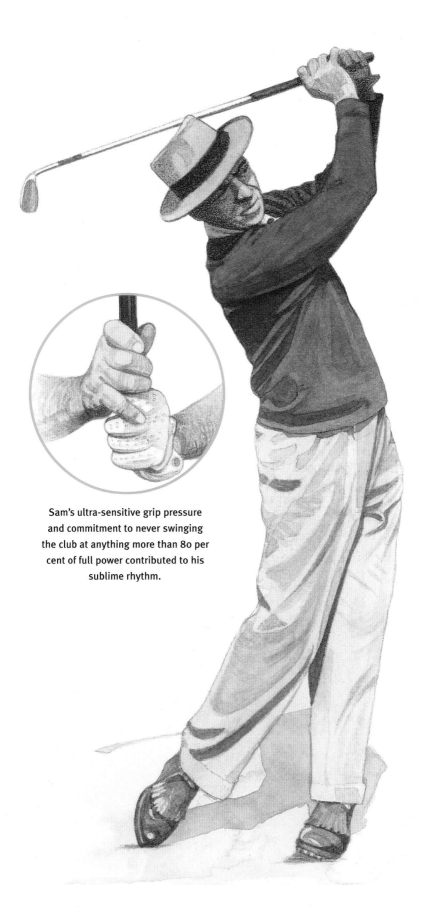

Sam's ultra-sensitive grip pressure
and commitment to never swinging
the club at anything more than 80 per
cent of full power contributed to his
sublime rhythm.

JH Taylor

Learning his skills on the links of the west coast of England, JH Taylor grew up to become one of the great wind players of all time and took part in many epic contests with his great rival Harry Vardon. It says something for the man's fortitude and skill that he emerged from battle with five Open Championships under his belt.

John Henry Taylor. His full name doesn't quite sound right, when throughout my lifetime he has been known by the abbreviation JH. Of all the three wonderful characters that made up the Great Triumvirate, it is perhaps JH Taylor who I knew most about. My first job as an assistant pro was at the Hallamshire, a lovely course near Sheffield in Yorkshire, where I worked for a gentleman called Willy Wallace who had himself been the assistant to JH Taylor. He told me many fascinating stories about Taylor, speaking with both admiration and fondness, so I got to know the great man rather well without actually meeting him.

Taylor had grown up playing his golf at Westward Ho! in Devon, a links he forever regarded as one of the greatest, and it was this wind-swept proving ground that would lay the foundations of a game tailor-made for championship golf. His swing was everything a successful wind-player could wish for – tidy, compact, punchy and very powerful – and during his dominant period he became renowned as a marvellous mid-iron player, strong and supremely accurate. He clearly had the temperament to complement those fantastic ball-striking skills, for he was barely into his twenties before he started making a major name for himself.

Indeed, at the age of just 23 Taylor stamped his authority on the game by shooting a then record score of 75 in the first round of the 1893 Open Championship at a wild and windy Prestwick. When one thinks of the primitive clubs and balls these golfers relied upon to express their skills, not to mention the relatively unkempt surfaces they would have had to play on, that must have been a marvellous round of golf. Torrential rain in the second round washed away his chances of victory that year, but in 1894 at Sandwich he drew on the experience of that loss to claim the first of his five Open Championship victories.

Taylor's big breakthrough was the beginning of a remarkable 20-year period that would be comprehensively dominated by the Great Triumvirate. Between them they walked away with 16 Open titles and they each would surely have won more had the First World War not intervened.

Taylor's talents extended way beyond the golf course. Although he came from a relatively poor and uneducated background, he matured into a real gentleman, articulate and well-known for his fluent public speaking. It was perhaps inevitable that he should become one of the most influential golfers of his era. Taylor felt in many ways that the life of a golf professional lay somewhat in the dark ages and he used his considerable intellect and persuasive skills to elevate professional golf to new heights. Such foresight and ambition were the building blocks of the PGA, an organization that Taylor almost single-handedly established. Professional golf never looked back.

The great writer Bernard Darwin, a fine amateur golfer himself, wrote that Taylor had successfully "turned a feckless company into a self-respecting and respected body of men." Quite what the other professionals would

have thought about the description 'feckless' is best not pondered for too long, but they were no doubt grateful for Taylor's pioneering attitude and vision for a better future for the professional game.

By any standards, Taylor's competitive playing career had been hugely impressive. He had every right to feel satisfied with his achievements and thoroughly deserved his 'quiet life' as the professional at Royal Mid Surrey, a post he held for the best part of 50 years. The life certainly agreed with him because Taylor lived to the grand old age of 91.

41: Sharpen the blow

DIAGNOSIS: The compactness of his swing, its punchiness if you like, was Taylor's hallmark. He wasn't as long a hitter as the other two members of the Great Triumvirate, but his tidy swing made him a very controlled, straight hitter of the ball – and that made him a formidable competitor.

As I said, for many years Taylor played his golf at Westward Ho! down on the Devon coast, where the wind would invariably have blown. And he wouldn't have gone far playing the high-ball game in those conditions, so it is fair to say that his environment would have been a contributing factor in him developing such a rounded and compact golf swing. His right elbow used to be especially tucked in throughout the backswing, which gave his swing that neat, no-frills compactness. It enabled him to punch the ball low and keep it under control. Such an

action would have generated a very definite and firm hit, the ball struck with real authority.

EXPLANATION: It's not uncommon for golfers' swings to develop according to the type of course they play when growing up. One doesn't see too many long and willowy swings from golfers brought up on links courses – that kind of technique just doesn't work.

Likewise, anyone brought up on a very tight golf course would have to learn to become a pretty accurate hitter in order to succeed and golfers reared on championship courses often develop into powerful hitters, but not necessarily the most accurate.

It must have been a fascinating spectacle to see Vardon and Taylor competing against one another, because the two men could not have had more

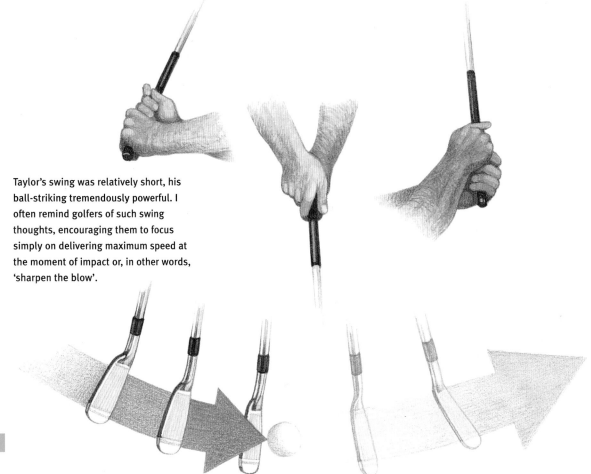

Taylor's swing was relatively short, his ball-striking tremendously powerful. I often remind golfers of such swing thoughts, encouraging them to focus simply on delivering maximum speed at the moment of impact or, in other words, 'sharpen the blow'.

contrasting techniques. Vardon with the long, lazy rhythm and the sweeping strike. Taylor with the compact, punchy action and the bludgeoning blows. There is a lesson in itself: to play one's own natural game and not be influenced by the play of others. All great golfers have been able to achieve this.

CORRECTION: Playing your own game is undoubtedly one of the key factors in making the most of your abilities. Taylor wouldn't have played any other way than his way, even when the conditions were far from linksy in character. Just as Harry Vardon would not have suddenly changed from a long, flowing swinger into a short, punchy hitter. Find an underlying style that suits you and try to let your golf swing evolve within that overall framework.

Valuable as that advice surely is, I think the most significant lesson we can draw from JH Taylor's game is the quality and authority of strike. It's something I frequently touch upon when teaching club golfers and the message is often conveyed in the simplest of terms: "Sharpen the blow," I say to pupils. "When you strike the ball I want you to sense there is real authority. It's not a slap, not a half-hearted prod at the ball. But a firm strike, Bang! Like you mean it." In offering such advice I make it very clear that I am in no way advocating a violent, overly aggressive swing of the club. But I think golfers who lack authority in the hitting area need to focus a little more on delivering maximum speed and energy into impact – the moment of truth. Sharpen the blow, just like Taylor used to. That's the key.

JH Taylor's swing wasn't pretty, but it was compact and powerful producing a low ball-flight that made him a formidable Open competitor and a five-time champion.

Peter Thomson

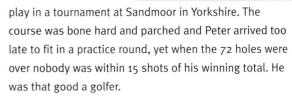

Here's a golfer who rarely used a driver for much of his career and yet won four Open Championships in the space of five years, then, when some considered him past his peak, he added a fifth title in the company of one of the strongest fields ever assembled.

How good was Peter Thomson? Well, how about that he is the only golfer this century to win three consecutive Open Championships. Or that when he won his first Open at Birkdale he used a set of clubs acquired from a manufacturer's tent on the eve of the championship. Can you imagine a golfer doing that nowadays? And then there's his astonishing record. The fact he won five Opens in total is impressive enough, but just look at his run of finishes from 1951 onwards. As you read it, please bear in mind that it starts when Peter was only 20 years of age: T6, 2, T2, 1, 1, 1, 2, 1, T23, T9, T7, T6, T5, T24, 1, T8, T8...we'll stop at 1967, but even into the 1970s he was still notching up top-10 finishes. It is a simply staggering sequence.

In his prime Peter was a good enough player to win any tournament he showed up at, but he loved fast-running courses and therefore links golf was his forte. Throughout his career he drove with a strong three-wood and he had a style of swing not unlike Sam Snead in that he aimed a hair right and as he swung the club down would turn his upper body 'into the ball'. He really squeezed the ball out and it would fly low and invariably bounce straight. As he once said: "I just happen to hit the ball low and straight, which is helpful at the Open." Not just at the Open, either. On one occasion I can recall he flew from the States to play in a tournament at Sandmoor in Yorkshire. The course was bone hard and parched and Peter arrived too late to fit in a practice round, yet when the 72 holes were over nobody was within 15 shots of his winning total. He was that good a golfer.

The first time I played golf with him was an exhibition match in 1951 at The Gezira Sporting Club in Cairo, where I was the professional at the time. Peter, accompanied by Norman von Nida, was on his way to England for the first time and that day shot a very tidy 67, the manner of which made me think he was a bit special. I went on to play a lot of golf with him over the years and I can tell you the best club in his bag was his temperament, no doubt about it. He was like Jack Nicklaus in that on the last few holes of a major championship with a chance to win he'd be the calmest person on the course.

He had a brisk, business-like walk, but there was nothing hurried about anything he did. He possessed an air of unmistakable self-assurance and as he marched from tee to green, often twirling a club in his hands, there were times when he had the look of a man who wondered what all the fuss was about. The spectators were more jittery than he was. "The super player," he once said "has one vital quality, calmness."

He had that all right – and much more besides. His swing had a wonderful, metronomic rhythm that never faltered even under the most intense pressure. His swing thoughts could not have been simpler. The set-up was his key and once that was in place he used to say "I just draw the club back and hit it." I remember he once phoned me when I was working at Sandy Lodge and said he'd like to drive up from London and get me to have a look at his set-up. He walked into the pro shop with a club under his

arm and when we stepped outside he said "I'm going to aim at that flagpole, I want you to check my set-up." So he did, and I said "it looks fine to me" and that was it, he didn't need to know anything else.

Because of his low ball-flight, the lush courses in the States weren't so much his cup of tea, but the really great players can turn their hand to any challenge and he still registered more than 30 top-10 finishes in the 90 or so tournaments he competed in on the US Tour in the 1950s. And remember, these were the golden years of Hogan, Snead, Demaret, Middlecoff and latterly Palmer. Peter can be grateful to fellow Aussie, Norman von Nida, himself a wonderful golfer, who managed to persuade him to turn professional at the age of 19, when at the time he was working as a technician testing rubber compounds for Spalding. Mind you, if he hadn't turned pro I have a feeling that Peter is one of those characters who would have been successful at whatever he chose to do. He could certainly have been a journalist, because there were times in his career when he would finish his round and head straight to the press tent – *not* for the obligatory interview, but to file his report to a newspaper in Australia. And when he went into politics I must say I thought he'd end up being Prime Minister of Australia.

After his competitive career on the main tour was over, he joined his old adversaries on the US Seniors Tour and in 1985 won nine tournaments and a then record sum of $350,000. The magic hadn't deserted him. Peter's golf game was like the Aston Martin car which he drove in the 1960s – once a class act, always a class act.

42: Be your own best course manager

DIAGNOSIS: I don't think there has ever been a golfer who managed his game better than Peter. He had an enviably simple, no-frills approach, right from the way he preached the virtues of a sound set-up, through to the way he plotted his way around the golf course always keeping the ball in play. One of Peter's gifts was that he knew his strengths and limitations. A classic example was how he so often refused to use a driver. You see, the manner in which he swung meant that he presented the clubface to the ball in a strong position – in other words, delofted – so the ball flew low and ran a long way. That made it difficult for him to flight a driver correctly so he seldom carried that club. Some might have considered that a distinct disadvantage and remodelled their swing in order to be able to hit a driver, but not Peter. He refused to change a swing which was perfect for 13 clubs, just to be able to use a driver. In Peter's mind, power always played second fiddle to position.

EXPLANATION: It's not the glamour side of the game of golf, but developing a shrewd sense of strategy that is the club golfer's most direct route to consistently lower scores and more trouble-free rounds.

CORRECTION: The purpose of the tee shot is to get yourself in play and in a position which makes your approach shot as straightforward as possible. The realistic aim of your approach shot is not to hole it, although that would be nice every once in a while, but to avoid possible hazards guarding the green and at the same time give yourself a holeable putt. And so it goes on. One smart shot benefits the next. I think if you were to go out in your next round of golf and play every hole with position, not power, in mind, you'll avoid the disaster holes and shoot lower scores. I really believe that. Above all, know your own limitations and play within them.

Position, not power, was Peter's philosophy. Even on a long par-five, three sub-200 yard shots played with control is all it takes to find the green in regulation. There's no need to fire all guns blazing off the tee.

43: Eliminate trouble down the left or right

DIAGNOSIS: A good round of golf isn't just about the great shots you hit, it's as much about the bad shots you don't hit. Peter knew how to stay out of serious trouble. Even when he did make a mistake it rarely became a disaster, he always seemed to be able to recover or at the very least consolidate. His equilibrium was totally unshakeable.

EXPLANATION: Other than talent, there are perhaps two main reasons why professional golfers are so adept at staying out of trouble. Firstly they understand the impact factors that produce certain shots. And secondly, they make smart decisions on the golf course.

CORRECTION: Let me give you two examples. First, a hole with trouble down the right – a scary proposition for the majority of club golfers. If you tend to slice your drives, I suggest you tee off with a three- or four-wood. It's got more loft and a shallower face, which reduces sidespin. So that means your normal swing produces less left-to-right curvature and thus helps keep you away from the trouble. If you insist on hitting a driver, tee the ball up higher than normal which encourages you to sweep the ball away with a slightly flatter, more rounded swing. That'll encourage a draw.

A hole where there is trouble down the left is less intimidating for anyone who tends to slice the ball, but it can still be risky. Bearing in mind that less loft equals more sidespin, it is advizable for the habitual slicer to go with the driver in order to promote a left-to-right ball-flight away from the trouble. A lofted wood could so easily pull the ball left, because loft nullifies sidespin and the ball will fly in the direction of your swing path through impact – remember, for a slice that is out-to-in and thus starting the ball left. For the golfer who shapes his shots with a natural draw, trouble on the left is a scarier shot. This time use the club you are most comfortable with, but tee the ball lower than normal as this encourages a more upright swing plane which tends to delay the squaring of the clubface and thus avoids the hook.

If there's trouble down the left side of the fairway, any habitual slicers of the ball should use the driver because less loft equals more sidespin, which allows your slice to take effect and work the ball from left-to-right away from the trouble.

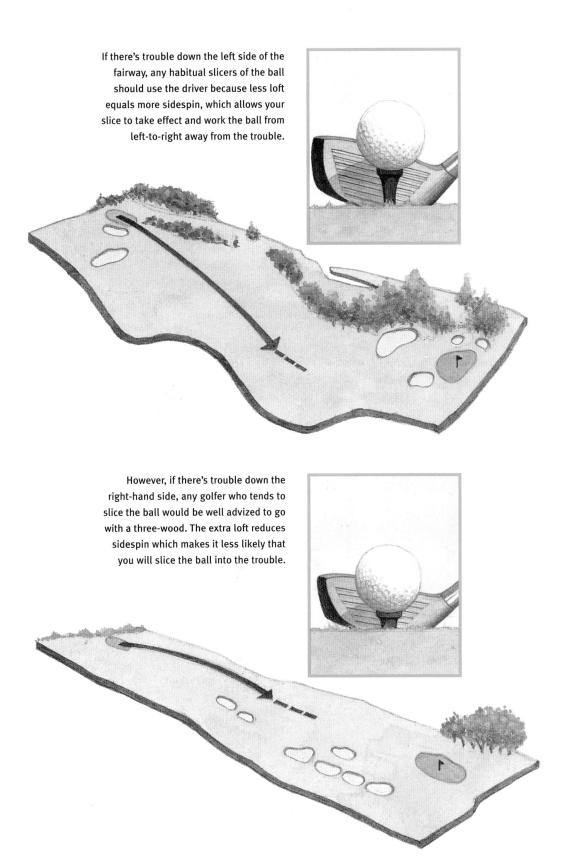

However, if there's trouble down the right-hand side, any golfer who tends to slice the ball would be well advized to go with a three-wood. The extra loft reduces sidespin which makes it less likely that you will slice the ball into the trouble.

Lee Trevino

Born into poverty, the grandson of a Mexican gravedigger, Lee Trevino could scarcely have had a less privileged upbringing. But he hustled and fought his way to the top, becoming one of golf's truly colourful characters, not to mention one of the most gifted.

Those who never witnessed with their own eyes Lee Trevino hitting balls should not be fooled by the less-than classic-looking swing, because make no mistake – Trevino was one of the most gifted ball-strikers ever. I would go so far to say that in the late sixties and seventies he was one of the four best golfers in the world. Jack Nicklaus once said to him: "You're a much better player than you think you are."

Lee climbed golf's ladder of merit the hard way. He started out collecting range balls six days a week, which allowed him precious little time to work on his game. When he left that job and joined the US Marines, a career perhaps not entirely suited to his outgoing personality,

Lee got probably the first lucky break of his short but hard life. A clerical error landed him in the Special Services division and he got to play golf every day with the officers. He became good, very good in fact, and after being discharged from the Marines was soon the professional at a club in El Paso, New Mexico. I got to know of him before he became famous and by playing with his own money on the line he soon became a lethal competitor. It was this kind of education that bought Lee a hard edge and a tough temperament.

Mind you it was 1968 before he made it on to the tour full time and by then he was nearly 30. Nicklaus and Palmer already had private jets and Lee was staying in cheap hotels and driving from one tournament to the next in a $1,500 station wagon, apparently frequently losing his way. A terrible sense of direction was not something he suffered on the golf course, though, and so impressed was veteran Gene Sarazen when he got paired with Lee at Westchester in 1968 that he came into the press tent afterwards and told the assembled media: "I just played with a man you're going to hear a lot about. He's going to win a lot of tournaments." Later that year at the Houston Open Lee had a great chance to fulfil Sarazen's prediction, but shanked a three-iron second shot to the last hole and lost to Roberto de Vicenzo by a shot.

When he eventually did win, he did so in the biggest possible way at the 1968 US Open at Oak Hill. On the final day, with Palmer playing behind him and Nicklaus ahead of him, Lee put on his lucky colours – red shirt and black trousers – and fired a 69 to win by a shot and become the first man in history to compile four sub-70 rounds in a US Open. When asked by the press what he was going to do with his $30,000 prize, he said: "I might buy the Alamo and give it back to Mexico."

He's a genuinely funny guy, good at seeing the humorous side of life and quick with the one-liners. He's also a private man, at tournaments preferring room service to the hubbub of a busy restaurant and content with his own company when he's bashing balls for hours on end with that well-grooved, repeating swing of his.

A low and obedient ball-flight meant that his game was made for links golf and he won his first Open at only the third attempt. That victory at Birkdale in 1971, when he edged out the virtually unknown Mr Lu – who ironically had beaten Lee 10&8 in a challenge match back in 1959 –

rounded off the finest month of his playing career. He had also won the US Open in a playoff against Jack Nicklaus and the Canadian Open.

At Muirfield the following year he birdied the last five holes in the third round, then on Sunday ruined Jack Nicklaus' best ever shot at the Grand Slam and knocked the stuffing out of Tony Jacklin. I think he was fortunate to beat Tony – even Lee said "God must be a Mexican" – but nevertheless it was impressive the way he played the 72nd hole after he'd chipped in and Tony had taken six on the previous hole. Lee could easily have got over-excited, but he kept his cool and hit the best drive he'd hit all week down the 18th and nearly knocked the flag out with his approach shot.

His high-stakes gambling days had taught him how to finish a man off and he never forgot. How else could he have won six majors, at a time when competition could scarcely have been stronger, and spread them over a 16-year span? When one thinks of the awful back trouble he suffered, not to mention the fact he was a relatively late starter on tour, it's a fantastic achievement. His name sits well in the highest company.

44: Impact ballistics determine the shots you can shape

DIAGNOSIS: Lee's self-taught swing might not be the prettiest to grace the fairways of the world, and it certainly has taken a punishing toll on his back over the years, but my word it is effective. He has a very open stance, swings the club back outside the line and then re-routes it on the inside coming down and keeps the club on line through the ball longer than any other golfer I've ever seen. Ouch, that hurts! All things being equal he hits a fade off the tee and in that sense he was like Ben Hogan, he could eliminate the left side of the golf course.

He could shape a shot any way he liked. I remember one particular example of his sublime shot-making during the Bob Hope Classic one year at the RAC Club in Surrey. The 18th hole there has a bank on the left and everything tends to kick right off there, and Lee hooked his second shot into that bank every time and the ball just followed the contours of the ground and ran on to the green. He was an incredibly inventive golfer and it spread through his entire game. Midway through 1984 he was having terrible problems on the greens. At the Dutch Open he decided to buy a Ping putter since everyone seemed to be using one at the time. When he went into the pro shop they only had one in stock and the lie angle was upright, totally inappropriate for his low-hands

Lee's distinctive swing starts from an open address position, from where he draws the club back outside the line.

The club never reaches parallel and the shaft points left. Lee's arched left wrist position means the clubface is closed, evidenced by the fact that the face is pointing to the sky.

As Lee starts his downswing he re-routes the club on the inside, which involves a quite pronounced flattening of the swing plane.

This enables him to swing the club into the back of the ball on a shallow angle of attack. Perfect for the driver. He then stays with the shot for longer than any other golfer, which keeps the club on line but is mighty tough on the spine.

If you're blocked out with only a short distance to the green, go with the draw shot. A slice simply isn't an option with a short iron because the large degree of loft makes it impossible to generate enough sidespin.

From long range you should always choose a slice in favour of a draw. It's easy to generate slice-spin with a straight-faced club.

style. He bought it anyway, took it back to his hotel room and banged it on the floor and stamped on it until the lie angle was flatter. The next day he putted beautifully and within weeks had won his sixth major, the USPGA, at the age of 44.

EXPLANATION: The way Lee hits shots makes him a fascinating golfer to watch. I remember being in Florida many years ago and admiring him as he hit full-blooded low-flying drives with a marvellous touch of fade. I noticed the clubface was distinctly shut at the top of his backswing. Then when he took his wedge and started peppering a target out on the range, I noticed the clubface was distinctly more open at the top of his backswing. The difference between the driver and wedge was night and day, so I asked him if he consciously made these changes and he replied: "I sure do."

CORRECTION: What is the relevance of that, you might ask. Well, where the ball goes depends on what the clubface is doing at impact.

Short iron shots reflect the swing path through impact, since there is minimum sidespin. Therefore an open clubface simply hits the ball higher – there's no sidespin, so there's no slice. Now since it's almost impossible to slice short irons, an open clubface with these clubs is useful. A closed clubface is detrimental, because there's a tendency to pull shots left of the target. A driver, with it's relatively straight face, produces more sidespin than backspin and therefore in the right hands it is easier to intentionally shape shots.

From the point of view of the club golfer, any lofted club is relatively easy to draw whereas to fade – which requires the necessary sidespin – a relatively straight-faced club is required. These factors have a major influence if you want to shape shots. For instance, if you want to go round a tree that's blocking your path to the green and you've only a short shot to play, you would not be able to shape the ball left to right because there would be too much loft on the club and thus too much backspin and too little sidespin. Thus from short range a draw is a better option because this shot relies on the clubface being closed to the swing path and, of course, a closed clubface means less loft and more sidespin.

If on the other hand you have a long way to go, it's difficult hitting a draw because as I've just explained in order to shape a ball from right to left the clubface has to be closed to the swing path. And since there is very little loft to start with on a long club, you only have to close the clubface a little and you've effectively got 'negative loft'. The ball therefore won't fly. Thus from long range a fade should be your preferred option.

Bear these impact factors in mind whenever you contemplate shaping an iron shot.

Harry Vardon

Dogged by illness for most of his playing career, it seemed that winning championships was the best possible medicine for Harry Vardon. He played a stylish game like no other golfer before him and had a reputation as a fearsome competitor. Together these skills brought him a record six Open Championship victories.

One of the greatest of all time and, one has to say, probably the greatest of the three golfers who made up golf's first triumvirate. My dearest friend Laddy Lucas was always talking about Harry Vardon, since he played a lot of golf with him as a boy in the 1930s. Vardon had a graceful golf swing and was what I would describe as the first upright swinger. Certainly when you look at the photographs of all the players of his generation and before, it is clear that they were very much rotary swingers of the golf club – or put another way, flat. To a degree the inferior clubs and balls of the period encouraged that kind of technique, as would have the restrictive clothing of the day – wearing a tweed jacket and a tie can't have been easy on the golf swing.

Like so many who achieve greatness, Vardon grew up surrounded by the game that he would later dominate. Born in Jersey in 1870, he caddied from a young age and watched his elder brother become a professional. By his early twenties, though, it was Harry and not his sibling who was sending shockwaves around the golfing world. In fact, in no time at all he was positively the man to beat.

Unusually for such a dominant force in the game, Vardon wasn't a strong individual. He suffered from tuberculosis for much of his lifetime and frequently competed in championships against doctor's advice. But he was a ferocious competitor and deeply dedicated. His great strength lay not in any muscular sense, but in the magical accuracy of his long game. The old story used to go that he hated playing 36 holes in a day because he would always end up in the divot holes he'd left in the fairways from the previous round. Actually he didn't take much of a divot with his iron shots, preferring to nip the ball sweetly off the fairway with great precision, but it was a good story, nonetheless.

Vardon's prodigious talent created an aura of invincibility that opponents found difficult to ignore. His great rival for so many years, JH Taylor, once said that there was no man he feared more than Vardon. Having been on the receiving end of a resounding thrashing at Ganton in the spring of 1895, Taylor's fears were well founded for in their first real head-to-head encounter in a major, the Open Championship later that same year, Vardon snatched the title from him in one of the event's first ever playoffs. In the years to come Vardon would go on to win the Open Championship six times, with victories spanning 18 years. He also found time to cruise across the Atlantic – something of an epic and time-consuming journey in those days – and claim a US Open title. In 1912, he was lucky he didn't get the chance to win a second US Open. Illness made it impossible for him to travel, which meant Vardon had to cancel his reservation on the maiden voyage of a certain liner called The Titanic!

Although Vardon's great rivals, JH Taylor and James Braid, along with the likes of Peter Thomson and Tom Watson, each got within one of Vardon's Open record, the longer it stands the more probable it

is that his remarkable tally of six will never be matched. Vardon's legacy to the game is more substantial than mere ink in the record books, though. He has the honour of being one of the few golfers to have a trophy named after him, an elegant statue awarded each year to the professional golfer with the leading stroke average in the United States. And he is unique in having a grip named after him – also known as the overlapping grip.

More than half-a-century after his death, then, Vardon's grip on the game remains as strong as ever.

45: The benefits of a 'soft' left arm

DIAGNOSIS: As I explained, Harry Vardon was a standard-bearer for a breed of upright swingers. However, this wasn't the only reason his swing stood out. It was equally significant for the presence of a distinctly bent left arm at the top of the backswing – markedly more bent than his contemporaries.

This gave Vardon's downswing effectively two hinge-points. By that, I mean as he accelerated towards impact he would straighten his left arm and straighten his left wrist, which meant that he created a tremendous amount of natural leverage in his swing. So despite being not an especially strong man, he hit the ball a long way. Imagine,

if you will, the action of throwing a Frisbee left-handed. That would convey the sense of how Vardon converted the energy of his golf swing into speed through the hitting area. I like to describe it as a lot of flow and throw, his loose, long and apparently lazy action effectively slinging the power out to the clubhead through impact.

EXPLANATION: Vardon always used to say that he loved playing against someone with a straight left arm, because he always felt that straight invariably meant rigid. He was almost certainly right. Golfers who try too hard to keep the left arm straight in the backswing do have a tendency to fall into the trap of keeping it stiff. And stiff means there is tension, the enemy of any golf swing. To my mind, there's no way of completing the backswing once tension has set in. Vardon perhaps went a little closer to the opposite extreme than would be advizable for the average player, but his example is a valuable one. And far from causing him problems, Vardon's bent left arm blessed him with a long, flowing golf swing that must have been one of the most effortlessly powerful of the day. Rather like a Victorian Fred Couples.

No golfer bent their left arm at the top of the backswing more than Harry Vardon. But it had its advantages. By straightening his arm in the downswing and uncocking his wrists he effectively had two hinge-points, which gave his swing tremendous natural leverage and lots of speed through the ball.

CORRECTION: Admittedly by today's standards, Vardon's bent left arm would be considered most unusual. Certainly not something a teacher could positively recommend to everyone. However his example provides us with a valuable lesson, namely that you shouldn't necessarily strive to keep your left arm ram-rod straight in the backswing. Some golfers can achieve it – Ernie Els is one such player who springs to mind – but you have to be tremendously athletic and flexible to do this. And sadly most of us mere mortal human beings can't fulfil both of those criteria.

This is why I like to see golfers allow for a little softness in the left arm, which usually manifests itself in a slight bend in the elbow at the top of the backswing. A little flex is no bad thing. Again, perhaps not as bent as Vardon's, but enough to allow the backswing to be completed. Seniors in particular would benefit from Vardon's example, by softening-up the arms and allowing the club to swing longer and fuller. If you can develop both the confidence to trust a longer swing and the rhythm to make it work, this can be an effective way for less flexible players to generate more clubhead speed through impact. The important point is that your left arm straightens at impact due to the centrifugal forces created in the downswing. This re-establishes the correct arc of your swing and thus obviates the need for any independent hand action to swing the clubhead freely and squarely into the back of the ball.

It goes without saying that Vardon achieved this in some style, as his superb follow-through and balanced finish illustrates so well.

Tom Watson

The brisk swing and the bouncy stride, the epic showdowns with Jack Nicklaus, the 10-year dominance of the Open Championship and for a time the seemingly bullet-proof putting stroke – Tom Watson will be remembered as a golfer for all the right reasons.

When I think of Tom Watson, qualities such as intelligence, inner strength and an extraordinary ability to 'putt the lights out' immediately spring to mind. In the late seventies and early eighties, this formidable collection of talents made him one of the few dominant golfers in history. I remember at the 1983 Open the bookies made him a 3-1 favourite – unbelievably short odds for a major. Mind you they were right to be nervous. One of the things that made Tom so good was that he could win when he wasn't on top form. "As soon as I knew I could win not playing my best," he once said, "I found it much easier to win." But Tom usually did perform to the best of his ability when it mattered most. Nothing flustered Tom. There was a calm confidence about him under pressure, as though he had absolute faith in his mental and physical prowess. The majestic, championship-clinching two-iron that he struck into the heart of the 18th green at Birkdale in 1983, one of the greatest shots I've ever seen, was a perfect example of this.

I recall Seve once saying that: "Tom is very tough, without question the most competitive of all my contemporaries." And I couldn't agree more. Certainly when I captained the Ryder Cup team at The Greenbrier in 1979, we all thought he was their top man. His wife was pregnant at the time and I remember hoping she would go into labour because it would mean Tom wouldn't play! When I went over to the practice ground, though, I saw that Watson's backswing was as flat as a pancake. I couldn't believe it. I was devastated when his wife did go into labour and Watson pulled out, because that was probably the only time in his career I wouldn't have minded him being on the opposing side.

A poor-swinging Tom Watson was a rare sight, indeed, though. No lesser man than Byron Nelson had smoothed out the rough edges in Tom's game and polished it for good measure. They'd got together in the mid-1970s after Tom had blown a couple of majors. Sitting down together before the final round of the 1975 Open at Carnoustie, Nelson told him: "Don't panic if you bogey some of the early holes. On this course, in this weather, they'll all have problems." The advice was spot on. Watson birdied the last hole as many of his challengers faltered. That got him into a playoff with Jack Newton, which he won the next day to claim his first major. Byron and Tom continued to work together for the best part of 20 years. "He's got everything," was Byron's simple diagnosis of Tom's game.

I can't argue with that. Tom was strong, an imperious iron player and a wonderful pitcher and chipper. But it was his putting that made him great. At his best, there was simply no one better. He was also wonderful at reading greens. I knew Tom's caddie Alfie Fyles pretty well and he told me that Tom used to walk alongside the line of a putt and feel the line through his feet (with my big feet, maybe I should have been a better reader of greens!) I watched him a lot when he won the Open at Muirfield on greens that I had always found difficult – there never seemed to be any obvious breaks, only very subtle ones. I lost count of the number of times Tom hit putts that I thought he'd missed, but within four or five feet of the cup it was as though the ball had eyes, the way it took the break and dropped into the middle of the hole.

Sadly for Tom, his putting deserted him when he was starting to swing the club better than ever. He was only in his mid-thirties, in theory a golfer's prime, and it must have been hard to stomach. But Tom is quite philosophical about it, as I would expect from such an intelligent man, saying that "maybe you can only go to the well so often with your nerves." It's an interesting point. With great players we grow accustomed to watching them knock in the three-footers with apparent nonchalance. But mentally it must take its toll over the years. After all, the same thing happened to another great holer-outer, Arnold Palmer. If Tom's putting stroke had stayed intact, who knows how many majors he could have

won. As it is, his name sits alongside Arnold Palmer in the list of all time major winners, below Jack Nicklaus, Bobby Jones, Walter Hagen, Ben Hogan and Gary Player – probably the best sixth place in history! He is not out of place in such illustrious company.

I must say if a youngster came to me today and asked me who he should model himself on, I'd have no hesitation in saying Tom Watson. Not just because of his swing, which I think was as good as anyone's throughout the 1990s, but for the way he conducted himself on the golf course throughout his career. He was never boastful in victory, never miserable or petulant in defeat. Indeed, if you turned up at a tournament to watch him walking off the last green, you'd never know whether he had won or lost.

What a great golfer ... and what a nice man.

46: Two parts to every good backswing

DIAGNOSIS: I remember sitting next to Tom at dinner in the build-up to the 1981 Ryder Cup at Walton Heath and him saying to me that he "couldn't hit his hat." When he asked me what I thought he might be doing wrong, I replied: "You must be joking, we're just about to play a Ryder Cup match!" Shortly after he'd won the 1983 Open at Birkdale, I was at Gleneagles when Tom arrived to play in the BBC's old Pro Celebrity series with Sean Connery. He walked towards me with an iron club under his arm and said to me, "Hey, what wouldn't you tell me at Walton Heath?" I asked him how he saw his game, to which he replied: "I want to hit the natural golf shape, a draw, but I just can't seem to at the moment."

EXPLANATION: This was Tom's most common swing fault. The reason he did that was because he delofted the clubface at address, and as soon as any golfer does that they're halfway to rocking and blocking. Tom couldn't hit a draw because there wasn't enough rotary movement in his swing. I grabbed the club from under his arm and said, "See that tree over there, set up to hit a shot straight at it." He did and sure enough the clubface was strong. As soon as he placed the clubhead behind the ball in a square-neutral fashion he started to turn correctly, which meant the relationship between his body and his hands and arms was a more evenly balanced one. In short, the club was now swinging on the correct in-to-in arc, imparting a slight draw.

CORRECTION: Tom swinging well is the perfect example of a relatively flat shoulder turn combined with an upright arm swing, which creates the perfect in-to-in arc. Some players deviate from this, but if I see a golfer deviate too far from orthodox, I often use the address position to change their swings. If someone is swinging too flat, I'll put the clubface in a strong position behind the ball, which encourages them to swing the club back on more of a straight line. Arnold Palmer played like this most of his career. On the other hand, any golfer with a tendency to swing overly straight needs the clubface neutral to encourage more rotary movement. It's important to be aware of these factors in your swing and recognize that sometimes you need to accentuate things to get back to orthodox.

Turn the shoulders in the backswing, clear the hips in the downswing.

47: Take the break out of short putts

DIAGNOSIS: At his peak Tom was one of the greatest holer-outers I've ever seen. It wasn't just the fact that he seemed to hole every short putt he looked at, it was the way he holed them. Bang! Straight in the back of the hole. You'd swear he was trying to dent the back of the cup.

EXPLANATION: Tom's entire short game was brisk and positive, so there's no doubt in my mind that banging in the short putts was very much his style. It was also a reflection on the amazing confidence of the man. As he said himself: "I was amazing. I aimed the putter and I knew the ball was going right along that line." He invariably gave the hole a chance with his long putts. If they didn't go in, he'd just bang in the return putt.

CORRECTION: The advantage of this style of putting is that it eliminates break on all but the most severe slopes. You hardly ever have to start the ball outside the hole. I think to a degree if you eliminate break on a putt, you eliminate doubt. So give Tom's method a try. Not on the first green of the monthly medal, but on the practice putting green so that you get accustomed to striking the ball more firmly from short range.

When he was winning his five Open Championships Tom was a fearless putter – loading his long putts with such pace that they always had a chance, and never doubting his own ability to bang-in the return putt.

Lee Westwood

The new millennium could prove fruitful for Europe's most exciting young player, certainly in financial terms and quite possibly in major terms also, because very few twenty-somethings seem as mentally and physically well equipped as him to land golf's ultimate prizes.

It is tempting to describe this talented young man as the next Nick Faldo and, although it would be unfair in the sense that Lee is very much one of a kind, it is accurate in as much as like Nick he possesses a rare mixture of special ingredients that suggest he could become a world-beater. Physically he is strong and his golf swing is sound, which enables him to harness that power and makes him one of the longest straight drivers in the world today. Mentally he's strong, too. Indeed, the old cliché 'an old head on young shoulders' rings true when I think of him. Confident without being bombastic; cool without lacking fire in his belly, he really has a great temperament. Even when he hits a bad shot he seems to be able to move on, he doesn't dwell on it.

The comparisons with Nick do not end there, either. They of course share the same country of birth and, amazingly were both inspired to take up the game of golf after watching television coverage of Jack Nicklaus at The Masters – Nick in 1971 and Lee in 1986. A half-set of clubs was top of Lee's wish-list that summer and within three years he was down to scratch – good, but not quite as good as the remarkable plus-four handicap he possessed at the time of winning the British Youths' Championship in 1993. As fine a time as any to turn professional.

It was soon after that when I first met Lee. He attended the European Tour's training week held in southern Spain at the start of every year, at which young 'graduates' starting out on their tour careers meet up with some of the game's more experienced figures, such as myself, and hopefully learn a thing or two to help them on their way. I must be honest, Lee wasn't spectacular to watch, just very sound of technique and receptive to advice – not that there was much of that necessary, since when I watched him hitting balls he was so orthodox that I distinctly remember saying to him: "Don't change a thing." It's funny because most years there's usually one golfer who really stands out from the crowd, but there were half-a-dozen very good hitters there that week and when I sat down with the rest of the training team one night and tried to identify the real star of the future, I really couldn't separate them. It was the same with Jose Maria Olazabal – obviously he looked good when he was a youngster, but there were lots of other good-looking players also and it's difficult at that early stage in a golfer's career to identify the extent of their courage and, quite simply, their ability to make the best of their ability. So yes, Lee looked sound, but then so did a lot of the others I saw that week.

His first few years on tour were steady, if unspectacular, but that changed midway through 1996 when he hooked up with coach Pete Cowan and his progress went from Ford to Ferrari-like in its velocity. His earnings went distinctly upmarket and exotic, too – nearly half-a-million to his name by the end of that season. Not bad for a 23-year old lad from Worksop. Being a shooting star is one thing, though, but sustaining that momentum and not crashing back down to earth is an altogether different proposition. Over the years I've seen many a bright prospect fade without trace. But not Lee. Far from it, in fact. Fuelled by success he embarked on one long, continent-hopping, smash and grab exercise, winning tournaments all over the globe and pairing up with Nick Faldo to complete a magnificent Ryder Cup debut. And the following season not even Monty's sixth straight Order of Merit title, a magnificent achievement, could prevent Lee being voted European Golfer of the Year.

The fact that he was able to build on that first taste of success and go on to greater things is yet another indication to me of Lee's phenomenal long term potential. He seems able to learn from his experiences, good or bad, and use them to positive effect. This will surely stand him in good stead when he sets his sights on majors. His debut performances were strong – top-25 finishes in both the US Masters and US Open – and I hope he capitalizes on this and wins a major nice and early. It is more difficult now than it used to be, but Lee is certainly good enough. He's a fearless player and such a wonderful holer-out, enjoying the enviable confidence of youth as he virtually puts a dent in the back of the hole from short range. He needs a little bit of luck to win a major, though – everyone does, to be honest. But given the opportunity I don't think he'll be found wanting. This is, after all, a young man with a soft spot for sports cars – a sure sign that rapid progress doesn't frighten him.

48: Don't spin your shoulders too early

DIAGNOSIS: Lee's swing is pretty orthodox right from the word go. He sets up to the ball nicely, although if I were to be hyper-critical he is perhaps a little crouched over the ball. But it does his swing no harm. He swings the club inside and upwards on the perfect arc, his shoulders turning as the hips and knees resist. At the top of the backswing, he gets into what I would call a real power position – the hands high, the shoulders fully turned and on a slightly flatter plane than the arm swing. The downswing is similarly impressive. I especially like the perfect synchronization as his arms swing down at the same time as the body begins to unwind. Then he really 'lets it go' through impact – a lot like Ernie Els in actual fact – flighting the ball with a natural draw created by a full-blooded in-to-in release of the club. And all in perfect balance. It really is great to watch.

EXPLANATION: Lee's coach Pete Cowan must take some of the credit for the way Lee's swing has matured and become more consistent in the years they have been working together. Particularly in view of the fact that none of the improvements have been made at the expense of Lee's natural ability to swing the club with great freedom and power. That's partly what makes him such an exciting player to watch and also why on a good day no golf course or opposition is too tough for him.

CORRECTION: So, what can you learn from this dynamic young Englishman's swing? Well first and foremost, it is an object lesson for any club golfer who has a tendency for the right shoulder to spin out too early in the downswing, throwing the club away from the body and outside the line. This is perhaps the most common fault I see at club golfer level and if you suffer from a slice off the tee this is more than likely the culprit.

If that sounds familiar, you should take particular note of how Lee swings his hands and arms down from the top. It reminds me of the great Harry Vardon who said that as he changed direction from the backswing into the downswing, he felt his hands swung down to hip height before his body even began to unwind. In reality, he combined the perfect arm-swing with the ideal body rotation, but his feeling was one of swinging the arms down first and this is a swing thought that would definitely help you if you slice. It encourages the hands and arms to play a more dominant role, swinging the club down into impact on the ideal path and plane.

Another effective way of stopping the body becoming over-active in the downswing is to hit mid-iron shots with your feet together. You may recall how Hale Irwin would occasionally spend weeks on end hitting balls in this fashion. As I said then, if it's good enough for a three-time US Open champion it's good enough for anyone.

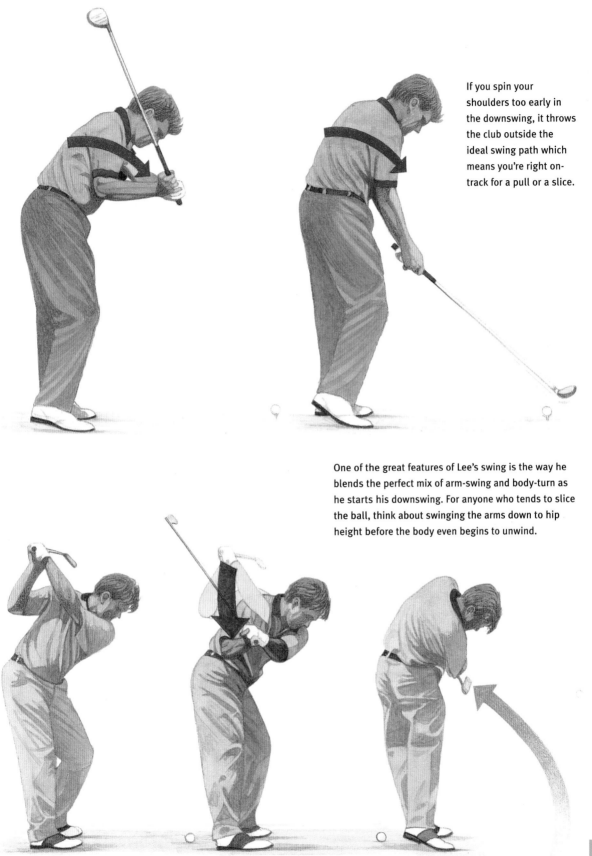

If you spin your shoulders too early in the downswing, it throws the club outside the ideal swing path which means you're right on-track for a pull or a slice.

One of the great features of Lee's swing is the way he blends the perfect mix of arm-swing and body-turn as he starts his downswing. For anyone who tends to slice the ball, think about swinging the arms down to hip height before the body even begins to unwind.

153

Tiger Woods

An alphabetical running order dictates that the last player featured in this book on the 20th century should, appropriately enough, also happen to be the man most likely to dominate the game of golf as it moves into the 21st century. Here's Tiger Woods, one of golf's millennium men.

How the game of golf has changed. At the start of the 20th century, when Harry Vardon ruled the fairways, professionals were virtually second-class citizens in the golfing world and there was as much money to be earned in making clubs with your bare hands as there was swinging them. Now at the beginning of the 21st century, golf's *numero uno* Tiger Woods can turn over a couple of million dollars almost as fast as he can swing his driver. And that's fast, very fast.

Nice work if you can get it. You have to have the talent first, though, and in that sense Tiger is fulfilling the pattern of sporting history whereby every now and then an athlete comes along who raises the bar, shaves a few hundredths off the stopwatch or in golf's case simply hits

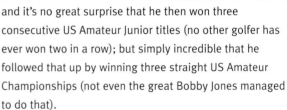

it further and shoots lower. Jack Nicklaus did it in the 1960s and I think it's fair to say Tiger's impact on the game is at least the equal. He's not reinventing the game as some suggest – no one will ever do that – but he is a phenomenon. Being introduced to golf before your first birthday itself almost defies credibility, but Tiger's exploits since then are just as mind-boggling. He starred on television at the age of two and shot sub-50 scores for nine holes at the age of three. At the age of five photographs suggest to me that he was swinging the club nicely and I know for a fact he had started drawing charts depicting the required trajectory of his iron shots. At the age of 13, when most kids are just taking up the game, Tiger broke par for the first time. He was light years ahead of his peers and it's no great surprise that he then won three consecutive US Amateur Junior titles (no other golfer has ever won two in a row); but simply incredible that he followed that up by winning three straight US Amateur Championships (not even the great Bobby Jones managed to do that).

Of course, the magnitude of these achievements were soon overshadowed when he won his first major, the 1997 US Masters. Records fell like nine-pins that week and only a lack of space on this page prevents me from recounting them in all their glory. What is more telling, I think, is that in his first 20 events as a professional on the US Tour he was 215 under par and six times in the winner's circle. That paints a picture of rare maturity and brilliance in one so young.

Long before then I'd been conscious of his reputation due to my regular visits to the States, but I'll be honest the first time I saw him play in the 1995 Walker Cup at Royal Porthcawl I was frankly quite disappointed with certain aspects of his method. With his short irons he swung the club too shallow into the ball which caused him to hit some out-of-control short irons. Mind you, the next time I saw him play at the 1997 Masters I remember thinking "my word, he's put that fault right very quickly." It was like he was hitting his short-iron shots off sandpaper, crushing the ball and spinning it tremendously. And, of course, he has that intangible ability to hole putts, which goes way beyond the realms of simply producing a good stroke. The great champions all have that gift. Add those qualities to his monumental power off the tee and it's hardly surprising that when he's on his 'A' game as he calls it, it's a case of who's playing for second.

But let's not get too carried away here. Golf isn't that kind of sport and there will be occasions when Tiger's game will explore more letters of the alphabet than a multiple-choice exam. I've read that Jack Nicklaus thinks Tiger will "win more majors than Arnold and him put together," which amounts to a total of 25. Jack is obviously paying the young man a generous compliment.

Without doubt when he's in full flow there isn't much I'd put past this remarkable young man. He wants success so badly, you can tell by the way he gets so irritated with himself when he's not living up to his sky-high standards. Mind you, he'll have to watch that side of his game and make sure it doesn't work against him. The new millennium will reveal Tiger's true colours.

49: Get 'behind the ball' and turn your back on the target

DIAGNOSIS: Tiger's fundamentals – such as the grip, posture and stance – are flawless, which is a great example to everyone. A lot of his power stems from this correctness, but also from his suppleness. He is blessed with an athletic physique which allows him to make an incredibly full shoulder turn with a minimal hip turn. This means the 'spring' is wound so tight in the backswing that when it unwinds in the downswing it releases prodigious speed and energy out towards the club. So he hits it miles.

EXPLANATION: Very few of you reading this will be able to reach the positions Tiger does in his swing. Indeed, his extraordinary talent and flexibility make him a rather dangerous man to copy. Most club golfers attempting to wind their upper body as he does, at the same time as resisting with the hips, would probably succeed only in a prolonged series of appointments with the local osteopath. But the whole point of this book has been to identify certain aspects of these wonderful golfers' swings

that can be integrated into the club golfers' games. So while you won't be able to turn exactly like him, what I am about to say will help you make a much better turn than you have until now.

CORRECTION: The first key is to get 'behind the ball' at address. Look at this image of Tiger and note how his head and upper body are behind the ball. By copying this you establish the correct angles at address – the right shoulder lower than the left, the spine leaning ever-so-slightly to your right. From this good set-up, try to feel that you turn your back on the target and as you do so swing your hands up above your right shoulder. This promotes the ideal blend of body-turn and arm-swing in the backswing. How much you have to release from the ground to achieve the full shoulder turn and correct setting of the club at the top will depend on the suppleness of your back muscles. Golf being the chain reaction that it is, you're more likely to make a powerful, on-line downswing from the correct backswing.

Get your upper body behind the ball at address, just like Tiger. Then turn your back on the target and swing your hands above your right shoulder to slot the club into a great position at the top.

50: You can't hit what you can't see

DIAGNOSIS: Tiger holes so many long putts it's incredible. Now, some of this is undoubtedly down to good fortune – I don't care what anyone says to the contrary – but at the same time it's also down to the great stroke he puts on the ball. If I were to be slightly critical I would suggest he has a tendency to be overly-aggressive. I read once that he "used to love to watch Tom Watson putt" which might explain why he sometimes hammers his short putts at a quite frightening speed. Tom did that in his heyday. But I worry about club golfers who try to always strike their putts so firmly. I mean, it's great when the ball hits the back of the hole, but when it misses… well, let's just say it leaves you with a lot of work to do!

EXPLANATION: Mechanically I can't fault his stroke, so let's focus on something positive that might help you hole more putts. One of the things I know he has worked on with his coach Butch Harmon is the position of his head, specifically making sure his eye-line is parallel to the target line at address, and also the way he looks at the hole. Perhaps you've not considered this, but I tell you it can make a mighty difference to the number of putts that start on the correct line.

CORRECTION: Next time you practice your putting, adopt your normal address position and make sure your eyes are over the ball by dropping a second ball from the bridge of your nose. If your eyes are directly over the ball I think you'll find it easier to see the line of your putts more accurately. And you can only hit what you can see.

Probably even more important than this, though, is to try to expect to hole putts like Tiger so obviously does. All of these great golfers can will the putts in – that to my mind is the real secret of putting.

Indeed, while every golfer in this book has his own style of swing they all show a phenomenal desire to succeed and a remarkable belief in their own ability. This is a fitting note to conclude on.

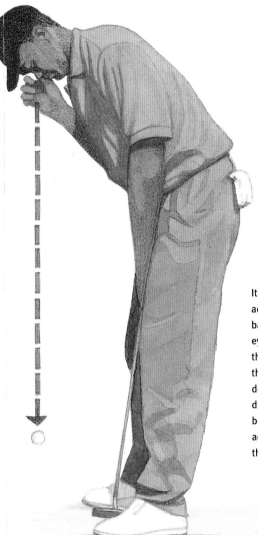

It's easier to get an accurate view from the ball to the hole if your eyes are directly over the ball. So rehearse this exercise which Tiger does from time to time, dropping a ball from the bridge of your nose and addressing the ball on the spot where it lands.

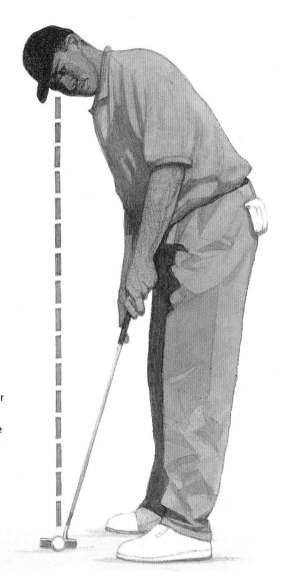

PICTURE CREDITS

Allsport: 36t, 97; David Cannon 26b, 27, 31, 62t, 63, 66b, 100–101, 138t, 138b, 146t; Stephen Dunn 50t,
Michael Hobbs 128t, 128b; Stephen Munday 22t; Stephen Powell 86b; Andrew Redington 9, 67, 74b, 150t;
Peter Taylor: 109; **Allsport/Hulton Deutsch:** 14b, 18t, 40b, 41, 108t, 118t, 118b, 119, 122t, 123, 129, 139,
Associated Press: 44b, 58t, 86t; **Golf World:** 55; **Hulton Getty:** 14t, 70t, 70b, 142t;
Phil Sheldon Golf Picture Library: 2, 7, 10–11, 15, 26t, 30t, 30b, 37, 40t, 44t, 51, 54t, 54b, 58b, 62b, 66, 71, 74t, 75, 78t,
78b, 79, 82b, 87, 92t, 92b, 93, 96t, 96b, 104t, 104b, 108b, 114t, 114b, 115, 132t, 132b, 133, 142b, 143, 147, 150b, 151, 154t,
154b, 155; **Popperfoto:** 18b, 19, 45, 59; **Ronnie Watts Collection:** 22b, 23, 36b, 50b, 82t, 105, 122b, 146b,
St Andrews University Library – Cowie Collection: 83